THE MYSTERY IN BEING A GYPSY

Gentylia Lee

Grosvenor House
Publishing Limited

All rights reserved
Copyright © Gentylia Lee, 2024

The right of Gentylia Lee to be identified as the author of this
work has been asserted in accordance with Section 78
of the Copyright, Designs and Patents Act 1988

The book cover is copyright to Gentylia Lee

This book is published by
Grosvenor House Publishing Ltd
Link House
140 The Broadway, Tolworth, Surrey, KT6 7HT.
www.grosvenorhousepublishing.co.uk

This book is sold subject to the conditions that it shall not, by way of
trade or otherwise, be lent, resold, hired out or otherwise circulated
without the author's or publisher's prior consent in any form of
binding or cover other than that in which it is published and
without a similar condition including this condition being
imposed on the subsequent purchaser.

This book is a work of fiction. Any resemblance to
people or events, past or present, is purely coincidental.

A CIP record for this book
is available from the British Library

Paperback ISBN 978-1-80381-879-5
Hardback ISBN 978-1-80381-880-1

ACKNOWLEDGEMENTS

To my friends and family for allowing our stories to be shared, much love and thanks.

My Aunt Julie, one of my favourite family members, for having faith, providing encouragement and for the continuous support you have given me.

Cllr Julia Wassell for the financial contribution that brought this book to publication, and for your friendship.

Allison Hulmes, My Welsh Kale Pen, for writing the foreword. I am so thankful our paths crossed. I treasure our friendship.

Professor Margaret Greenfields, for her kind recommendations for editing, proof reading, and continued support.

John Chadwick for his personal donation towards the book cover design costs.

Jo Luman, Pauline Anderson, Michelle Gavin, and W.R. Smith for your reviews.

Multiply, who fund the project 'Skills Impact' which brought me in contact with Vicky Nash. Vicky is an excellent adult tutor. A person who owns the ability to ignore stereotypes, who instead takes every new person, her work position brings her in contact with, at face value. "Vix thank you for going above and beyond."

To George Monbiot, for allowing me to use your article, and Duncan Campbell and Jim Davies for your contribution.

CJ Gardiner, for enhancing my photos.

Thank You All.

Book Reviews

Throughout my 20 plus years in education I have read many educational books but have struggled to find something that captures the lived experiences of the Gypsy families that I have had the pleasure to work with and call my friends.

This author takes the reader on her family journey outlining the difficulties Gypsy children can experience at school to working with professionals in social care, housing, and policing. Alongside this is the history of the Gypsy Holocaust which wrongly is just a footnote within the secondary curriculum at some schools. It is essential that this knowledge is preserved and shared with young people, so I am delighted that Genty (Gentylia Lee) has become an author.

I highly recommend this book to all professionals not just those that support Gypsy children and their families but all teachers who have the opportunity to challenge prejudice within society through education.

– Jo Luhman - Headteacher of Kings International College.

Even from the title of this book, I was hooked. The intimate portrait of the author's family unfolds, with characters as rich as any country people in a Thomas Hardy novel with their rich language, humour, and fascinating day-to-day family lives. It might not surprise non-Gypsy readers to learn about the strong culture and powerful family bonds, these are synonymous with Gypsy life. However, it might come as more of a surprise to learn that most families have lived in houses and not trailers (caravans). So too might it surprise people to read of the love of education and learning, and knowing now that Genty has become an author confirms her love of both researching and writing.

What strikes me most however is the subtle and not-so-subtle racism that pervades society and which the author and her family, like so many others, have had to learn to live with. She describes how the parents of children in the school behaved towards her and her family. A familiar story to me I am afraid.

What strikes me too is how her family have responded over the years with dignity and honour this makes heart-breaking reading.

This is a book that needed to be written it is a gentle insider view of a Gypsy family and is a million miles away from the sensational TV programmes we have become used to now-a-days. Which denigrate our community and stereotype us. Making it easy for society to continue the mockery and racism which we experience every day. Genty's is a voice that needs to be heard it is our history, our culture, and our present. It is what has made her who she is today – a strong but gentle woman with a beautiful story to tell. If you want to know about a real Gypsy family, if you want to get a true insight whilst laughing and crying then read this book.

– Pauline Anderson OBE, BEd Hons, Director of Learning, Inclusion and Skills Derby City Council, Chair of Travellers Movement.

'The Mystery of Being a Gypsy', is a wonderful account of the author's life and experiences. This is a tender, brave, honest, and gorgeously written autobiographical account of her life as a Romany-Gypsy woman. Her narrative keeps you turning the pages at speed; greedy to know more. As the book progresses, we are shown how prejudicial and racist legislation has been passed against this ethnic group. This piece of work is a great social documentary and should be shared widely with educators, schoolteachers, and those in decision-making positions across public life and civil society. If you want to educate yourself and understand the truth about Romany-Gypsies, history, and heritage then this book is compulsory.

– Michelle Gavin Head of Business Development FFT.

This book provides a unique insight of the historical discrimination Romany-Gypsies have received. The author gives her personal lived experience of the discrimination, trials and tribulations faced whilst demonstrating her resilience in adversity.

The book documents the author's progress throughout her own life. She has been able to maintain and develop her own cultural identity and was forthcoming about her ethnicity. The author promotes an educational approach towards those not belonging to the ethnicity, thus beginning to challenge discrimination in a positive manner. Such an approach helps break down cultural barriers and sets good foundations for all to build on.

The author highlights the historical wrongdoings not just in the United Kingdom, but across the world. The prejudices directed solely toward an ethnic minority group included "nowhere to call home" to the atrocities of the "lesser-known" attempts of the Nazi to eradicate the Sinti/Roma/Gypsies during the Holocaust. The book also shows the history of the government's involvement, who implemented new laws, that in today's society would be seen as racist.

As a mental health practitioner, I am curious to know how detrimental the constant discrimination is to an individual's personality formation. In a society where interpersonal relationships are frequently fractious because of fears held about Romany Gypsies, a lack of tolerance, conscious or unconscious bias held or even children being bullied because they are born to an ethnic minority group; it all shapes our identity and builds a framework for adulthood. Some may be more vulnerable to depression, paranoia and even suicide.

The author introduces a rich understanding of why Romany-Gypsies are possibly the last race in which it seems to be openly acceptable to be racist, and she has highlighted the importance of breaking down prejudice for populations, races, and creeds to live in harmony together. A highly recommended must-read!

– W. R. Smith Bachelor of Science,
Honours Degree (BScHON).

A call to attention

This book portrays authentic Romany-Gypsy voices and ways of speaking which may appear to some readers to be ungrammatical. This is not so however, as with any other form of community-specific speech for example Patois, there is a rhythm and accepted rules of grammar and use and my ethnicity is the same, when speaking in English, rather than Romaness (Anglo-Romany – Pogardi chib).

Throughout my writings there will be noticeable dialect differences i.e., Grandfarver instead of Grandfather. The capitalisation used for my Dad, Mum and others who are import in my life (as my personal show of respect) and in direct contrast lower case being deliberately used where there is ordinarily a capital, i.e., nazi (again, as my personal preference, which is intended not to validate or show respect with capitalisation).

I have used Italic writing when sharing my thoughts and views. To empathize a word, I have placed the word/s 'inside' single quotations.

Some names have been changed to protect the identities. However, my family and friends' names have not been changed.

All first- and second-hand accounts of our experiences are factual, there has been no sensationalising.

Foreword by Allison Hulmes

I was honoured and humbled to be asked to write the foreword to this astonishing autobiography by Gentylia Lee (Genty). It is no hyperbole to say that this is one of the most important books about Romany-Gypsy life that I have read.

First and foremost, this book is important because it is written by a Romany-Gypsy woman. Too few books have been written from this perspective and we need to hear the authentic lived and living experiences of Romany women whose lives have been treated by Gorger writers (non-Romany writers) as peripheral and one dimensional. Genty's personal story paints a picture which is alive with nuance, depth, and the vital role that Romany women play in achieving justice and equity for our people.

From the very start of her life, Genty has been a born leader, a listener and problem solver. All qualities that have clearly been nurtured in a warm, secure, and loving family. Genty's leadership and advocacy is the golden thread which weaves throughout this book, and I was also touched not only by the strength of it, but also by the ability of so many of the Gorgers she has had dealings with, to reflect and learn from their contact with Genty. This is a gift and something vitally important for us all to learn in the magic which Genty possesses to take people on a journey with her. The phrase 'you catch more bees with honey' kept coming to mind as a phrase which could have been written for Genty.

Ultimately, this book is a seminal read for anyone wanting to genuinely understand the impact of a lifetime of being exposed to stereotype and racism, which is built into the fabric and structure of society in the UK. It is also a ground-breaking read for anyone concerned about the over-representation of Gypsy, Roma and Traveller children looked after by the state, who are removed from kinship care, from culture and ethnic identity. Too many of our families live with the intergenerational trauma caused by this severing of our families, acts of state brutality from which we don't recover. We need to understand the impact from those directly involved so all social workers, social work students and policy makers should read this book and be educated on how transformative the outcomes for Gypsy, Roma and Traveller children are when they remain cared for within ethnic culture and kin. Genty's story gives us hope that we can achieve this, and we have to listen and learn.

The final lesson that Genty gives us is that all we need to know to close the inequality gaps which persist for Gypsies and Travellers is to give up space, listen, let us speak and let us be leaders of the changes we need to see.

Thank you Genty pen.

1

GRANDFARVER CHRISTMAS

I had never dreamed or desired to write a book, my passion was to find the answer to my Dad's question, "What did the Romanies (Gypsies) do, that was so horrific, it has resulted in us being despised worldwide?" I began to research to find the answer, and in doing so 'my persistent inner voice' continuously prompted me to share publicly what I have learned and experienced, my inner voice won. This is my story....

I had a wonderfully happy childhood and was raised with many extended family members. I lived on a site (Gypsy caravan site) with my Mum's side of the family from the time of my birth up until the age of four. Most of my memories from childhood, that I can recall, are from living in our house. I have a single memory of living on the site.

I was lying in bed on Christmas eve, in 1979, feeling very excited and a little nervous. I was willing myself to sleep because I knew Father Christmas doesn't leave presents until all the children are fast asleep.

But it was too late I could hear bells, he was here, and I was still awake! I can remember squeezing my eyes tightly shut. In the mind of the then four-year-old me, I believed if I couldn't see Father Christmas, he wouldn't notice that I was still awake. Even though I knew Father Christmas had landed on our site, I didn't even dare to sneak a peek, until my Mum came in giving me permission to look out of the window.

But when I did, I couldn't see the reindeers or the sleigh, but I did see Father Christmas; I saw him walking through our site ringing a bell.

I jumped straight back into bed and fell asleep. The next morning my 6-year-old cousin Wayne, who was looking very pleased with himself, informed me that he'd seen Father Christmas.

"Did you see him too?" Wayne asked.

I told him, "Yes, I saw him, and he had left us so many presents."

Wayne stated, "It wasn't Father Christmas it was Farvie dressed up, he was ringing his handbell – you know - the one with the wooden handle up the trailer."

I didn't believe Wayne, not for a second because I'd seen Father Christmas with my own eyes, and also my Mum had told me it was him.

Wayne was telling lies to torment me, he was only having a joke and I knew this for sure!

We had moved from the site into housing, before the arrival of my baby sister Sarah. The opportunity arose because there were empty houses in the street where my Dad's family were already living. My parents preferred to still live near family members and in our street from number twenty-four (which was our house) to number forty, where my Dad's Uncle Tommy and his family lived, there were eighteen children - all of us cousins. We spent so much time together growing up.

We all attended the same local primary school, shared the same hobbies (gymnastics and swimming) and we were always outside together playing. I could write a book just about our childhood adventures. From standing with our Guy Fawkes, doing 'Penny for the Guy' to throwing lumps of wood up into the tree in the hope of getting the conkers to fall - which resulted in lace-less shoes and hours of competitive fun. We'd build dens for hours and there was an old shopping trolly that we used as our very own roller coaster cart. Our days were filled with fun and laughter, playing together, falling out, and obviously making up and being best cousins again.

I loved primary school especially because my teacher, Ms. Kimberly, had singled me out as her pet. It was back in the days of miniature glass bottles of free school milk and the sharing of the fruit that we had brought in from home. As an adult I can understand why Ms. Kimberly liked me, it was because of my generosity. But this was not an unusual trait in our family because

THE MYSTERY IN BEING A GYPSY

growing up with our cousins, we had always shared our sweets and our toys. It was never an option to not share. Ms. Kimberly was a beautiful lady with a jolly character who had glowing red cheeks and the perfume smell of cigar smoke.

"Who would like to share their apple?" Ms. Kimberly would ask.

And I would, every day, be a willing volunteer by raising my hand. I loved being able to share my apple and it did not matter who with a girl, a boy, a black-skinned child, a white-skinned child, or any other shade of skin colour in between. This is the beauty found in all children they do not see or know about these so-called differences. Children do not see skin colour or know about ethnic, creed, or cultural differences either. It's a simple case of playing together due to the similarities in game play preferred.

Arriving in class we would place our apples on the table, which had a large sheet of paper laid out on it that served as a tablecloth. We would draw a circle around our apples and write our names next to them, and that's where they'd be left until the morning break. As a reward for sharing, aided by Ms. Kimberly, we were allowed to cut our apples in half. When Ms. Kimberly helped me to cut the apple, I would feel such a grown-up little girl being able to use a knife. I can recall it took a lot of effort pushing down through the apple until successfully cutting it, never quite equally, in half.

For those of us that shared nicely we were allowed to take our half and gift it to a child who hadn't brought any fruit into school. Ms. Kimberly could be as strict as she was kind, but she was certainly a righteous lady. If any of the children in her class were reluctant to share, when they had been asked to do so, Mrs. Kimberly would take their apple, cut it 'equally' in half and then give it to a child without fruit. She ensured every child in her class had a snack to eat during morning break. In my family, sharing was an expectation rewarded with praise, no schoolteacher had to teach any of my Mum's children how to share, we already knew how to.

I'd choose the bigger half of my apple to give away and I am sure this didn't go unnoticed by Ms. Kimberly. I would often gift a girl who I felt sorry for because most of the other children, in my class, wouldn't sit next to her. She smelled quite bad, and her clothes were very worn. She was a quiet girl and gifting her the apple was never met with a smile or a thank you. I can remember her hair looked as though it wasn't brushed, and she always wore her hair down. I took notice of this because I had to wear my hair in neat plaits every day because Mum didn't want me to catch head lice.

Even when I begged my Mum to go to school wearing my hair down, I was not allowed. She'd say, "No! You'll get joobs."

Ms. Kimberly, well before the days of the 'no-touch policy' (that we are seeing more of in schools now) scooped me up into her arms, twirled me around and upon standing me back onto my feet she announced, in front of the entire class, "You are a kind girl you."

I was made to feel special by her. She was an amazing schoolteacher, a prime example of excellence, she rewarded kind behaviour and good manners above academic achievement. She also had the common decency to treat children, as all humans should be treated, as individuals, and without prejudice. As a child I just enjoyed being in her class but as an adult, I can fully appreciate what a wonderful teacher she was and just how important the schoolteacher's role plays in the lives of their pupils.

My school, Lessons Hill Primary, in Orpington, Kent was situated next to a special needs school. Our playground adjoined their cafeteria which had a full glass panel wall. My cousin Wayne and my sister Kathy would often spend their playtime trying to communicate with the children from the neighbouring school by playing a charade-type game with them. My Kathy, Wayne, and I often spoke about how good it would be to be able to play with the children from the school next door.

Wayne had decided, one particular playtime, that the children from the neighbouring school should indeed come out to play with us!

THE MYSTERY IN BEING A GYPSY

I was sat on the playground floor watching Wayne trying to communicate through his miming actions. He was trying his best to tell the children if they went to the double door and pushed down on the bar it would open (in doing so this would leave no barriers between us). Wayne had been trying to communicate for a while, children would come and go, some would shake their heads to tell him, "No!"

Others didn't have the capacity to understand, and many were simply enjoying their dinner.

I was busy brushing off the tiny pieces of grit that were stuck to the backs of my legs from sitting on the playground floor when I noticed a boy, from the special needs school was responding to Wayne. This boy understood perfectly Wayne's miming actions asking him, "Do you," - pointing his finger at the boy, "want to play with us?" Wayne slapped himself on his chest, then pointed in the direction of my Kathy and me.

The boy nodded enthusiastically, and his face lit up with delight. Not only did he understand he wanted to come out and play with us too! Wayne signaled for the boy to go over to their cafeteria door, using both his hands he mimed how to first grip and then to push down on the bar. I got up and stood next to Wayne who was repeating his miming actions.

Three girls had come over to join the boy, but I am not sure if they understood what we were trying to pull off. The boy was trying his best to push down on the long bar, which ran the full width of their cafeteria door, with his three giggling companions alongside him. It was just the technique that failed him, it was clear to see he was using all his might to try and click the bar down to open those dividing doors.

"Yes, Yes, Yes," Wayne shouted in encouragement, which had made a few other children in our playground take notice. Kathy and I had joined to mime-communicate with the girls, willing them to help the boy to push down on the bar. Other Lessons Hill pupils were laughing with excitement and several of us spontaneously began clapping as encouragement for the boy to get the door open.

Sadly, at this point, we had caught the attention of our dinner supervisor Mrs. Janker, and our little group was then quickly dispersed by her actions, similar to shooing chickens away. All the excitement and fun and the opportunity to play with the children from the special needs school had ended abruptly.

As a result, for a long while after, we were not allowed to wave at them because we were directed to play at the other end of the playground, by the dinner supervisors thereafter. It was our punishment for wanting to play with the neighbouring children. Mrs. Janker was a dinner lady who supervised our playtimes, a mother of a child who attended Lessons Hill, and a person who kept company with the 'in crowd'. Which was a clique of mothers, who would congregate in the school playground at drop-offs and pick-ups to have a gossip. Mrs. Janker's son Martin was in the same class as me and I learned from him that his mother's account of what went on in the playground (on the day she worked as a playground supervisor), had become quite a subject matter to gossip about.

Martin 'my informant' told me what his mother and, what the other mothers were saying about the Gypsy children's defiant and unruly behaviour. Old Janker had stigmatised us as naughty Gypsy children.

Martin declared, "I know all about what you have done – 'you' were naughty."

And for the record, I did not like that Martin had said, I was being naughty because there was no intent to be naughty in school or anywhere else for that matter, as my Mum was extremely strict and did not tolerate any type of brazen (naughty) behaviour. I 'knew' my Mum would have told me off if I would have been brazen, and she didn't! Mum simply explained that children with special needs had their own school and their own playground to play in to keep them safe.

Mrs. Janker did not like me and my relatives very much, and it seemed as if being a Romany-Gypsy child, helped old Janker to form unjust negative judgments. Her watchful eyes and loose tongue aided her to hold conversations about us (the Gypsy children) with the other mothers in the playground.

THE MYSTERY IN BEING A GYPSY

A few weeks later, when the bell rang for home time, I had raced out of class to see what flavour ice-lolly my Mum would be holding, (we got ice-lollies, every day, when the weather was nice).

I was an intuitive child and had a negative gut feeling which had stopped me dead in my tracks. Standing still, I looked around for my Mum. But she wasn't standing in the playground, at the top of the slope, where she would normally be waiting for my sister Kathy and me. I scanned the playground and finally spotted her standing with 'that' group of mothers which included Mrs. Janker. I sheepishly made my way over to them. As I got within hearing distance, I heard my Mum giving an open invitation to anyone who wanted to visit our home, "They'd all be welcome to do so."

I didn't have a clue what was going on and I was so confused as to why my Mum would invite Mrs. Janker, and those other women, to our house. I felt a little sense of betrayal at hearing my Mum inviting them to our home. Mrs. Janker of all people! After all she was the person stopping us from being able to wave at the children from the school next door.

Walking home from school, I was listening to my Mum telling my Aunt that she had overheard the age-old belief, held by many Gorger people (Gorger: a word from our language, that means anyone who is not a Romany). Mum had over-heard these women speaking about, a centuries-old, common stereotype that Gypsies are dirty. With relief, I learned my Mum had not invited the other mothers into our home for a social visit.

Instead, she had offered for these women to come and look around our house to conduct a 'Cleanliness Inspection'. Mum had given the women an offer for the opportunity to see for themselves if this stereotype was true about us. She had invited them, individually or together within their group, to come back to our home and see for themselves the standard of our living conditions.

However, this offer came with a condition!

7

In return my Mum would then visit their homes to conduct the same inspection. Mum had laid down the ground rules that the inspection should certainly be a thorough one, this would involve pulling out fridges and washing machines to see if it's clean behind them.

My Mum does not credit top clean, and she made it known that to verify their belief that Gypsies' homes are dirtier than Gorgers' homes, it should be put to the test by inspecting areas that are not on show!

My Mum had walked over to the congregation of women, close enough, to be within ear-shot, and this was the reason she was not stood in her usual spot to pick us up. She was ready and waiting to catch them speaking about her daughters and nephew over the recent playground incident. I had told Mum 'Everything' that Mrs. Janker's son Martin had told me. But my Mum would not approach Mrs. Janker directly about what Martin had told me, because she felt that could get Martin in trouble for what he had conveyed to me. So, instead Mum had positioned herself close enough to hear their conversation hoping to catch them gossiping about the playground situation. But instead, she overheard their views and opinions about Gypsies in general; her spontaneous offer that would put their theory to the test was my Mum's way of dispelling this stereotype - that certainly bears no resemblance on us as a family.

Strangely enough, none of those women chose to accept the offer! They all apologetically stuttered in their defense that they didn't mean us as a family. In their view, we were not Gypsies because we lived in a house; a feeble excuse when considering every Romany-Gypsy child in that school lived in housed accommodation.

Many people who believe they know about my ethnic group can hold a preconceived notion that Gypsies are just culturally living nomads! This incorrect belief makes it nearly impossible to convince such 'believers' that Romany-Gypsies are a legitimate ethnic group.

When I am subjected to hearing: "You can't be a Gypsy," (followed by whatever else) I already know I am about to be exposed to conscious or unconscious bias, negative stereotypes and possibly, even some blatant racism thrown in - just for good measure.

A year after my birth in 1976, Romany-Gypsies were legally recognised as an ethnic minority group in the UK and gained protection from discrimination under the Race Relations Act and the Human Rights Act.

2

CHILDHOOD ENCOUNTERS

As a child, I struggled immensely with both reading and spelling, I could not understand how some words were phonetically spelled when others were not. However, my handwriting and art skills from an early age were quite good and I loved socialising at playtime with my school friends and cousins. I disliked the coldness of the assembly hall and sitting on the floor, but I was extremely interested when listening about God. My sister Kathy and I also attended Sunday school regularly, not because my family belong to a religion but simply because it was a routine Sunday activity that we enjoyed.

Yet for me, it had sparked an interest in those magical stories such as Jonah living inside the whale's belly and the strength of Samson. That story I could relate to because I had long hair, and fantasising about having magical strength because of the length of my hair was easy for me to do. My absolute favourite was the story of David defeating the great and nasty giant Goliath, such biblical stories intrigued and captured my imagination. Somewhere along the line, that I cannot recall 'how' or 'why', I also learned about nuns, who dedicated their lives to God. I had adopted this notion and would sit after having a hair wash, in front of a mirror, using the towel my hair was wrapped in arranging it around my face to look like the headdress that the nun's wear.

I would take great delight and pleasure looking at my reflection in the mirror, I believed that because I looked like a special child of God that must mean I was. At the grand old age of 6 I had decided that when I grew up, I was going to become a nun!

I had an amazing childhood with loving parents who made us feel loved, safe, and special. We were raised on good old-fashioned

THE MYSTERY IN BEING A GYPSY

home cooking and on the weekend, we would play outside with our cousins while the meat and bacon puddings were cooking. We'd eat our dinner, then go back outside to play, weather permitting. We all knew our boundaries and did not dare to cross them. With either my Parents, Aunts, or Uncles constantly checking on us. We were looked after by the adults, and we also looked out for each other. My childhood had plenty of fun such as early morning trips in the summer to the seaside, we would go to theme parks, and the fairs, and our family tickets to go to the circus, just as soon as they arrived, were bought.

My Father was a very calm, kind, caring and extremely righteous man. He owned the ability to make our day trips turn into an adventure. My Dad preferred family time then going to the pub with the men. Throughout the summer every weekend we would be off to the beach and to my mother's dismay, (as we loved the musical Mary Poppins and we knew every word to each of the songs), we'd sing one song after another from the film, as we travelled, making sure to include 'Supercalifragilisticexpialidocious' several times over.

Our Father would convince us that the car was breaking down and no matter how many times he repeated this trick, telling us that we may not make it to the seaside, we still fell for it. He would say, "The car is an old banger," and we really believed that singing 'Chitty Chitty Bang Bang we love you' as loudly as we could, would magically help the car reach our destination. Finally, after singing our hearts out to encourage the car to get us to the seaside, my Dad would announce, "Your singings worked girls the car is going to get us there!"

Mum took the opportunity to relax, and she well deserved it. I am not just saying it, but she is my real-life superwoman. Her endurance and ability to work, run the home, cook every evening, keep the most sensational gardens and spotlessly clean home is second to none. My Mum has always worked hard without complaint and on our seaside trips, she would enjoy sunbathing and reading her favourite 'Take a Break' magazine. She was a child who struggled to learn in school and despite her best-efforts reading was a task she did not master well. She picked up on her reading skills during her adult years. My Mum was failed by the school system and her years of schooling were not beneficial for her.

There was a male teacher in my Mum's school, who sounded to me as though he was more like a drill sergeant in the army than a teacher in a children's school. He would routinely inspect the children's shoes to see if they would meet 'his standard'. Mum's shoes were worn, and she dreaded her teacher's forthcoming, Monday morning inspection. She was around seven years old and for the want of both trying to please him, and so as not to be shown up, she decided to paint her shoes. Finding a tin of light blue paint, in her parents' coal bunker, she got to work painting them in the hope of making them look shiny and new.

Arriving at school the next day, with her newly painted shoes, Mum felt embarrassed because she had not actually managed to make an improvement. So, she changed into her plimsolls and hid her shoes inside her desk. There was a boy, who would often accompany the teacher on these inspections: 'The Little Chad Kisser' (as my Mum references him) and he would be present, wearing his very own shiny shoes. When they reached my Mum, the teacher asked, "Where are your shoes?"

Mum pretended that she had forgotten them, only to have 'Chad kisser' tell the teacher he had seen her place them inside her desk. The teacher told my Mum to get the shoes out and reluctantly she did so. She has often shared with me the memory of feeling 'Ladged to Death' (extremely embarrassed) because the teacher had laughed at the sight of her shoes which gave way to the domino effect, where all the children joined in with his parni-taking (mocking laughter).

Mum is nearly 70 now and it is self-evident how childhood negative memories can certainly last a lifetime. Such treatment resulted in serving my Mum to enable her to become a strong and resilient adult. She is used to hard work, has a strong mindset, and is a selfless person with a heart of gold, who will help a stranger if she can.

It is worth noting that there were many children, both Romany-Gypsies and Gorgers alike, who had worn hand-me-down clothes and shoes back in the 1960s. I am not sure if this teacher just delighted in mocking children, but he certainly made them aware that they were beneath his materialistic standards, (Gorger: non-Romany).

THE MYSTERY IN BEING A GYPSY

Both my parents had also attended Lessons Hill Primary in the early 1960s. Back then what was the Special Needs School, when I went there, was their infant's school. And what was our Primary School, used to be their seniors (Secondary School).

On my Mum's first day in Primary School, she was walking back to her classroom in line with the rest of her class after assembly, when her teacher held her hand up (like a traffic policeman would do when giving the signal for a motorist to stop), and she then asked her name.

My Mum replied, "Betty Baker Smith."

With this information her teacher instructed her not to enter the classroom but instead to stand outside. There was no explanation or reason given to her. The teacher walked into the classroom with the other pupils leaving my Mum obediently obeying her to stand outside.

Louie, who is my Mum's first cousin, saw her standing outside as she walked past with her class. She asked, "What are you doing out here Bet?"

Mum told her what had happened, and Louie informed her she had the worst teacher in the school because she was known to hate all the Gypsy children. My Mum, who was a five-year-old little girl, had been made to stand alone outside the class, on her first day!

Her physical features: having dark curly hair, olive-brown skin and being petite had caught her teacher's attention and the shared surname with her cousins, had served to conclude her suspected ethnicity. My Mum's cousin's ethnicity had already been assumed because they lived on a trailer (caravan) site. This assumption made was not because their parents or the children themselves had ethnically identified because they all knew better. This teacher believed….

Actually, I do not know what she believed. I cannot relate with, nor do I understand, any adult who has prejudgments towards children because of their ethnicity, creed, or skin colour. Least of all can I comprehend how a teacher would be able to justify, in their own heart and mind, standing a small child outside the class, on her very first day attending school, for no other reason than the ethnicity of which she was born!

This form of punishment was used frequently in schools when teachers would send unruly, defiant, naughty, or disruptive children outside to exclude them. It was a punishment of isolation, an act of segregation, that separated these children from their peers. Yet, this was not the case for my Mum, she was 'othered' purely because of her ethnicity. Her punishment would have influenced the other children in her class to believe my Mum was trouble. It would have been seen as wise for the other children to keep their distance from Betty Baker Smith, after all, she had been made to stand outside the class on her first day, which meant she must be trouble - Right?

Othering (noun) The process of perceiving or portraying someone or something as fundamentally different or alien. Based on the conscious or unconscious assumption that a certain identified group poses a threat to the favoured group. Othering is largely driven by politicians, media, and people in positions of authority.

During my Mum and Dads primary school years it was common for the Gorger children, in the school playground, to taunt the Gypsy children with the following song:

My mother said, I never should,
Play with Gypsies in the wood;
Grave were the dangers, so said she,
Keeping company with the Romany.
My father told me I never should,
Play with the Gypsies in the wood;
Grave are the dangers he would say,
Because Romany steal all children away.

I have had no luck finding the origins of this song. However, I did come across accounts of Gorgers online who remember singing it and whilst they share different variations, the above is the one my Mum remembers. Her peers would regularly sing this song to her and her relatives, throughout their 'System Education' years.

THE MYSTERY IN BEING A GYPSY

The innocence of children who know no better can always be forgiven but the original author and more importantly the playground supervisors, who allowed this to be repeatedly sung at the Romany-Gypsy children cannot be forgiven so easily!

It seems this racist rhyme has existed for at least two centuries in England as well as Scotland. Constant daily bullying impacts a child's ability to learn and sadly it's a common practice to hear that the majority of Romany-Gypsy children, who have racially identified, or whose ethnicity is self-exposed because of living on a Gypsy caravan site, have experienced continuous bullying in one form or another.

The statistics speak for themselves and there are many references that evidence how people suffered depression after bullying starting in school which has been very common for the Romany-Gypsy children whose ethnicity was known.

My Mum's younger brother Jimmy and a couple of her male cousins were constantly in fights at school. My Uncle Jimmy had a few Gorger friends who would stand by him and his cousins, against the barrage of bullying that they endured. The verbal and physical assaults that took place happened regularly. Teachers on duty in the playground did nothing to control the situation nor did they intervene to stop the fighting; they instead participated as onlookers.

My Uncle Jimmy laughs when sharing memories of his school experiences, he has a good mentality of forgiveness towards these children, who are, as he understands a product of their environment and upbringing. Just like my Mum he has managed not to carry a victim status but instead can see the comical side of it all. When laughing about his many childhood fights, which he was provoked into having, or where he had defended himself – the way he tells these stories will make all listeners laugh.

He told me, that as soon as they said the words, "Dirty gyppo" he was ready to have to fight! When speaking about those supervising teachers though, he doesn't laugh so much.

Those adults, I believe, must have felt that the Gypsy lads deserved the abuse. Who knows, they could have even enjoyed the fact that the Gypsy lads had to fight against larger groups of boys. His teachers would routinely stand watching them fight and did nothing to intervene. No matter what or who caused the fights, the outcome would be the same for my Uncle Jimmy - he would be made to stand or sit in a corner with a dunce hat on his head. As bad as this may sound, we all laugh when hearing about his dunce hat wearing days, it is our inherited warped sense of humour which is better than the alternative; to become angry or cry.

It seems unbelievable that such forms of psychological punishments were inflicted on children by so-called intelligent professionals.

If you are too young to know what a dunce hat is, do take the time to look it up.

To continuously be on the receiving end of this form of punishment could easily break a child's spirit but somehow against all odds it managed to ignite a warrior spirit in my Uncle Jimmy. Yet, I can't help but wonder just how many adults who suffer from an inability to control negative emotions do so because of the mistreatment they endured, in their early years, within the school environment.

I have listened to my Mum share, many times, her memory of sitting at her desk trying her best to read a book. Mum still relives how she was concentrating so hard, trying to understand what she was reading as she had once again told me about this memory. She had not heard her teacher calling out her name, her classmate sitting close by said, "Betsy" and just as she raised her head to look up, a piece of chalk hit her directly in the eye; her teacher had thrown the chalk at her to get her attention.

My mum defends this teacher saying, "She didn't mean to hit me in the eye though, but my God it did hurt."

Her eye was painful and streaming for the rest of the school day and she wasn't sent for medical care either.

I cannot imagine this did anything to help my Mum with her reading struggles and concentration, and I do wonder, "What was that teacher thinking?"

THE MYSTERY IN BEING A GYPSY

My Dad never told us many of his childhood memories, I know much more about my Mum's childhood. I do know he was a bright child and picked up learning well. I know he passed his eleven plus (an exam taken that decided academic ability which could be make or break either going to Secondary modern school or Grammar school with set pathways).

One story I can recall him telling us when we were children, that he told again and again right into our adulthood, which never failed to make us bust (burst out laughing) was about his P.E teacher. Now though, as I am writing this, it evokes only sadness to recall it. Because my Dad is no longer here with us, and I will never again be able to listen to him sharing any of his memories. But also, because in all honesty, there was nothing funny about what happened to him, other than the way my Dad told it, making it humorous.

He had forgotten his shorts and his P.E teacher told him to go to the lost property room to collect a pair so he could participate in the Physical Education lesson. He did as he was told and when looking through the clothes in the lost property room, he could only find one pair of shorts that he noticed were soiled so he left them behind. Returning to the teacher, he lied and said there wasn't any there because he felt ladged to tell the teacher that the shorts were, "Shitted right up."

As children knowing shit was a word we were not allowed to use, his use of the word alone would make us bust (burst out in laughter).

The P.E teacher told my Dad to follow him back to the lost property room. Where he picked up the same pair of shorts that Dad had already left behind and then his teacher gave him an order, "Go and put them on."

Dad protested that he could not wear the shorts because they were dirty. Whilst holding the shorts in his hands, he pulled apart the waist band so the teacher could view them for himself.

Yet again he was ordered to put the shorts on, even though this teacher knew my Dad was telling the truth, that the shorts were absolutely disgusting!

He knew my Dad wasn't refusing to wear the shorts, to either, get out of participating in the physical education lesson, or to be disobedient. This teacher could see, with his own eyes, the reason for his refusal. My Dad then unflinchingly told his teacher, "I'm not going to put them on and if you try and make me, I will go home to tell my father."

Dad knew his father (my Grandfather Joe) would not allow him to wear those shorts. His teacher replied, "You need do as I say, the shorts are perfectly suitable for a forgetful Gypsy who's not remembered to bring in their shorts."

He then walked away leaving my Dad alone without any care to check if my Dad would carry out his threat to return home or if he would stay on the school's premises. My Dad, true to his word, ran out of school to go home and told his father what had happened.

My Dads shoulders would go up and down, whilst he laughed when telling us, that he had told his Dad, "Father I couldn't wear them shorts coz someone's shit themselves in them". We would hold our stomach muscles, in laughter at this point in the story, even though we'd heard it many times before.

My Grandfather Joe drove him back to school; they walked straight into the P.E hall. Grandfather's opening line was, "Who do you think you are?"

Without waiting for a reply, he followed on with: "My child's not an animal, used to living like a pig."

The teacher was immediately apologetic. Grandfather informed him that his son had never worn filthy, unhygienic clothes in his life, and he would not be wearing shorts with feces in them no matter who tells him to.

This teacher knew his behaviour was unacceptable, and once faced with an adult Gypsy man, he quickly changed his tune, singing his apologies!

What this teacher learned, contrary to his own conscious prejudice, that led him to believe it was okay for my Dad to wear a filthy item of clothing was - that it was not! Grandfather had confronted the teacher to inform him that in fact, it was offensive and insulting to tell his son to wear soiled shorts.

For this teacher to believe that shorts containing excrement were suitable for a Gypsy pupil to wear, his prejudice could never be justified!

The above photo is of my Grandfather Joe Buckley and his baby brothers. John is sitting on the back of the horse, and Tommy is sitting at the front. My Grandfather was 16 years-old in this photo which was taken in 1930.

Our family are certainly not accustomed to wearing filthy and unhygienic clothing! The reason that this event even took place was because a person considered to be a suitable professional in authority to teach was a complete bigot! All these incidents that took place in school to each of my family members have proven to me, what I was raised to know - academic qualifications cannot make a person a good professional nor can academic qualifications make anyone a decent human being either!

Sharing my Dad's memory in writing has failed to make me laugh like it once did. As I said, "It was only my Dad's entertaining skills that made us laugh at this situation." Could you imagine how you would be feeling if this happened to your child in school? Can you imagine a teacher ordering your teenager to put on soiled shorts? Now try to imagine your child telling you that their teacher would not listen to their protest because he believed the shorts were suitable for the likes of your child, due to their forgetfulness, and their ethnicity.

Bigot: a person who strongly and unfairly dislikes other people, a person who hates or refuses to accept the members of a particular group such as a racial or religious group.

Just like all the prejudices my family members were subjected to by professional teaching staff, when they were defenceless children, none of it is a laughing matter! The laughter that took place was because of the skill of a father, who like so many other people from our ethnicity, came to learn that laughter is the best therapy. My Dad wasn't just good at making light of a bad situation, he had an excellent ability to understand and forgive, rather than to judge and hate. The world is certainly a less rich place in his absence.

It is truly devastating that the world is full of so many people who have hatred in their hearts against those who do not belong to their own ethnicity, creed, or colour; in 2018, the Equality and Human Rights commission survey revealed that more people openly expressed negative feelings towards:

Gypsies, Roma, and Travellers - 44%
Muslims - 22%
Transgender people - 16%
Gay, lesbian, and bisexual people - 9%

People aged over 70 - 4%
Disabled people with a physical impairment - 3%.

I am fortunate to have so many fond memories of my happy childhood with storytelling, playing games and home cooked food being at the heart of all my favourite memories. We were quite indulged children, given the era, to be able to have so many family day trips and to be able to also participate in our hobbies. The memories I have of spending time at the beach are treasured. We would build huge sandcastles that were the biggest on the beach! Our Father's seaside trademark would be to hand-scoop the sand from around our sandcastle, creating a moat. We would then go to-and-fro to the sea with our buckets to collect water which we'd pour into the moat.

His second trademark was to build a huge sand turtle, with detailed patterns drawn on its shell. We would delight in having the best sandcastles on the beach, made by 'Our Dad'. We'd spend hours digging holes and burying each other in the sand. My sister Sarah was such a happy, giggly little girl, she had a larger-than-life character, and she is still the same as an adult, owning our father's skill to entertain. My Kathy and I would pretend to be stuck in the sand and my Sarah, being much smaller than us, would then try with all her might to help pull us out. Even though it was physically impossible for her, she would believe it was her help that brought the success.

A child's innocence to believe is a beautiful thing in an environment where they are cared for. My childhood was for sure, one of wearing rose-tinted glasses made with love. In the real world though, outside the safety, warmth, and comfort of my own home, I encountered the ugly side of humanity.

3

CHILDHOOD MEMORIES & ADULT DISCOVERIES

Growing up my Mum would teach us (my Kathy, my Sarah and me) the words in our language that she knew. I must emphasise there are many different dialects of the Romaness (Romanus/ Romani) language. Pronunciation and spelling can also vary within the different dialects. With the long-standing 'othering', 'open bigotry', and the 'incursions' against our ethnic group, it is a sorry tale that the English Romany (Romanichal, (Needies) have lost our teaching and therefore our ability to speak our native language.

Many from my Grandparents generation would sparingly speak their native tongue. Speaking in English helped to reduce the threat against them, as concealment of their ethnicity was necessary to prevent being unjustly targeted with hate and discrimination. My Grandparents' generation were obedient not to speak their native chib. Within just two generations, through attrition, our beautifully fluent Anglo-Romaness language became broken - Pogardi chib.

As a child, I only knew just a single fluent sentence alongside many words, "Kakker rokker nixxies," - which is a warning sentence to - "be quiet and not to speak."

But, as a child, I seldom knew the reason behind the warning, it was simply a rule to be respected. Over the years especially between my Grandparents' and Parents generation it became fashionable for books to be published containing words from our language, largely authored by the Gorgers who befriended the Romany people that they had learned from. I have been raised not to teach strangers our sacred language, and I have wrestled with my own mental argument whether to include some of the words I know but the deciding factor, which swayed my decision, was to remind myself there are now Gorger people who have studied our language and know it better than I do.

There is also 'literature galore' containing and translating our Anglo-Romaness, written by both Romany and Gorger people which is widely available. The importance in sharing the single fluent sentence above (that I grew up knowing) is to evidence how detrimental speaking our language was because it helped to expose our ethnicity. Many practices were adopted to hide our ethnicity. We are an ethnic group skilled at the heart of surviving and adapting, which has helped ensure our existence. Even in present times, there are Gorgers who place themselves in a privileged, self-appointed position, justified by the education they afforded, who sell our stories, history, and language for their own monetary gain. Many of whom, especially academics and historians have also produced research papers, much of which were brought about using confirmation bias.

Confirmation bias: Owning a tendency to process information by looking for, or interpreting, information that is consistent with their existing beliefs.

As a child I never knew being born a Romany was reason enough to be hated because my Parents, Grandparents and wider family were good at protecting us children. I can honestly say within our family home I do not have bad memories. We were protected from the outside world. I lived in our family home until I was nineteen years old and only witnessed one single argument, with raised voices, between my parents. As a middle-aged woman now, I can fully appreciate and admire the love and respect my parents had for each other, and the love they hold for us. Mum nurtured and catered to our every need including our Dads; he was treated and idolized as our King. Between Mum, Kathy, Sarah, and I we waited on him hand and foot, and he appreciated and deserved it all.

Mum was strict, and we would not dare overstep the boundaries that she put in place. She would speak to us with her eyes, and we would know right from wrong from her glance or glare. She made our home, what can be best described as a 'homely' home.

All the children (our relatives and friends – Gypsies or Gorgers) loved being in our home, it was always packed with other children.

The best quality we were raised with was to hold no prejudice towards others. All children, of any culture, social class, ethnicity, colour or creed were welcome in our home. Both Mum and Dad taught us that all people are individuals and that there are good and bad in all walks of life. Many of our Gorger friends chose to address our Mum as "Mum". She has many unrelated Gorger and Gypsy children who have chosen to call her Mum, or in her later years Granny and my Dad was certainly a Father and Grandfather figure to many - and I think this speaks for itself.

My negative memories, as a child, are as a result of being in the school environment. One such occasion took place in the dining hall when I was nine years old. It was a terrifying experience for me. My Kathy and our cousin Wayne were both in their last year of primary school at this time. There are just 17 months between me and my Kathy and that's the reason I can calculate my age accurately. I was sitting next to a girl called Baily Longhurst. We were friends and always sat next to each other in the school dinner hall. Baily was the type of child who always ate every morsel of food and dessert and would go up for daily seconds.

Baily regularly asked to have the food that I left, and it became a habit for me to offer her foods I didn't like, or I did not want to eat. Spoonful by spoonful I would pass over the food from my plate to hers before I began to eat. It wasn't an easy task, but I knew I wasn't allowed to share food utensils with anyone who wasn't an immediate family member. This is a regulation I have been raised with because of my Mum's hygiene standards. I knew not to drink or eat behind anyone, and I certainly knew not to allow my cutlery to touch Baily's plate either.

Mrs. Janker was covering the dinner and playtime duty. She would walk up and down the hall whilst we were eating. I had finished my dessert by the time Baily had just started hers, she had done a good job of eating her food and most of the food I'd given her. The dinner lady, who serves the food, called out for anyone who had finished their dessert, and wanted more, they could come up for seconds. I happily got up from my chair to join the queue.

THE MYSTERY IN BEING A GYPSY

It was rare for me to get seconds, but it was my favourite sponge pudding and hot custard (even though the school one wasn't nowhere near as good as my Mums homemade one). Just as I got a second helping of dessert Mrs. Janker came up behind me and took the bowl out of my hand without saying a word. She was holding the hand of a sobbing Baily, and I was ordered to go back to my seat.

I watched Mrs. Janker walk Baily over to the teacher's table where she was then seated and given my dessert. I could see Mrs. Janker was talking to Baily, who was sitting nodding her response, in between taking giant mouthfuls of my sponge pudding, but I couldn't hear what was being said. The Janker then came over to me, picked up Baily's plate with her leftover food on it, placed it down in front of me and said, "Now finish your food."

I looked down at Baily's plate that had 'her' knife and fork on it and replied, "I am not eating Baily's left overs."

The Janker then came around to my side of the table, she grabbed my arm and physically pulled me up out of my chair. Her quick actions startled me, and her tight grip hurt. I began to cry.

Very quickly, my Kathy and Wayne were up from their table and standing by my side. They started pleading with Janker to let go of my arm because she was hurting me. This staff member had such a tight grip around my arm that later in the day bruises appeared. I was scared and I became even more trashed when my sister started to cry. Janker ignored our tears, and our pleas for her to let go of me.

As she dragged me near the entrance doors of the dining hall, she commanded my sister and Wayne to stay where they were. I was so frightened that I cried out for my Kathy and Wayne to rescue me, pleading with them, "Don't let her take me away, please."

And that was a real fear for me, at that moment, because my Mum had told me that there are bad people in the world who take children away from their families. All I knew was that this Janker was a bad person, and I didn't know where she was trying to drag me off to. I was beside myself. I reached out with my other hand and got a grip on the dining hall door handle in my brave effort to save myself.

It all took a theatrical turn when Wayne kicked off and hit Jankers' arm repeatedly while shouting at her, to let go of me. My Kathy took hold of my other arm, and for a moment we were in a bit of a tug of war against the Janker. Suddenly she let go of me and stormed off, I felt instantly safe in the embrace of my sister's cuddle. Both my Kathy and Wayne were also emotionally upset. In no time at all Janker had returned with our Headmaster who had already decided we were to miss out on our playtime. We followed him behind and adhered to his instructions. Which was to sit outside his office in silence. In those days, children did not have a voice and punishments would be given without being questioned.

Later in the day when the bell for home time rang, I ran out of school because I could not wait to tell my Mum about what had happened, I knew she would go stone raving mad when I told her. After explaining what had happened, with my Kathy's input also, I pulled my arm sleeve up to show off the fingerprint bruises. My Mum marched straight into the school and headed towards the headmaster's office, without knocking she burst into the room and told him straight.

I felt vindicated when my Mum announced, "I am going to do to 'your' staff member what she's done to 'my' daughter."

My Kathy and I voluntarily sat down on the chairs outside the office, the same chairs we sat on during our lunch break. The Headmaster was pleading with our Mum to calm down and he closed the door to speak privately with her.

Mum was told that Baily was upset about not being able to get seconds because she had not finished her first round of dessert and when the dinner lady had invited the children for seconds Baily had tried eating her dessert as fast as she could, she was so worried about not having seconds this had made her cry. Mrs. Janker had approached Baily whilst I was queuing for seconds and asked why she was crying. Baily told her that I had given her my food to eat which made her slower finishing her dessert and now she was going to miss out on desert seconds.

I'm not sure if Baily made it sound as though she did not ask for or want my food, or if that was just the Jankers' interpretation of what had happened. But either way, I was the one who paid for the lie, it was put across to our Headmaster that I had somehow 'made' Baily eat the food I did not choose to eat.

Mum retaliated telling the Headmaster, "I don't care what she has done no one puts their hand on my child!"

He promised to deal with his staff member and to be fair he must have, because Mrs. Janker never put her hands on me again – in fact she never addressed me, for any reason, ever again. A silent and unspoken agreement existed, whereby, we didn't acknowledge each other.

There was even a bonus, we were once again allowed to wave to the children from the school next door because after this incident my Kathy, Wayne and I went back to having the full use of the playground.

Most of my time at Lessons Hill Primary was spent being happy and progressing with my learning. When I left primary school, I went to Walsingham Secondary school for a brief period before we moved. On my Kathy's first day at Walsingham, she was placed in a classroom with children who had learning difficulties and/or behavioural problems, alongside every other 'known' Gypsy pupil.

My Kathy felt this classroom environment was intimidating because it was full of much older pupils, some of whom would have been in their last year at school. However, there was some fun to be had by partaking in the lesson on how to make and throw paper planes, one my Kathy didn't need a lesson in because our Dad had already taught us how to make the best paper jet aircrafts. However, it wasn't intended for us to play 'how far can a paper plane be thrown' at school.

The known Romany-Gypsy pupils regardless of age, behaviour or academic ability had all been placed in this classroom which was completely segregated from all the other pupils and did not teach the set curriculum. When my Kathy came home, she told our Mum they had all been pretty much left to their own devices. There were no set lessons or extra teaching staff to support the pupils.

One teacher had supervised around twenty-five to thirty pupils of all ages, some of whom needed different types of support.

My Kathy explained her teacher was extremely interested in learning about our ethnicity and she had spent some of her time having a chat with her about it. Mum didn't need to hear any more and announced to my Dad, "I will not be having this! I am not sending my child to school to teach the teacher."

In true 'My Mum's Style', she went into the school the very next day, without having made an appointment and made sure her child wasn't kept in a class where she would not receive even a basic level of education. When my Kathy went back to school the next day, she had to sit tests, and from their results, she placed middle and top for all future lessons – which also earned her a prefect badge!

I used our Romany-Gypsy Guild Facebook group to find out in what year our members had a similar or the same experience as my Kathy did in school. I wrote: Were you placed into a segregated class, for Gypsies only, or for children with behaviour and learning issues, and if so, what year did this happen?

From the replies received we can estimate a time frame, where the apartheid classes were certainty operational, in England, for at least 50 years. From the 1940s through to the 1990s. Romany-Gypsy children were routinely denied receiving a curriculum standard education, by segregation.

But for years both prior and since, our children have been taunted and bullied out of the education system altogether. Yet, in today's society there is a stereotype that is believed about the people termed 'Gypsies and Travellers' (wrongly as a collective) which depicts us as having a cultural tradition to not engage our children within the education system. This couldn't be further from the truth and there are no more or less, within our ethnic group, who do not value education than there are to be found in any other ethnic group.

There is also another struggle to be had, which is against those with the mindset who believe children can only be educated within the state school system. Elective Home-schooling is commonly frowned upon in wider society by certain partisan people. All children should be treated fairly and should be able to access and obtain an education, within the system, without having to face racial bullying and teacher low expectation. Racial bullying is a huge problem which so many Romany-Gypsy children face, and certainly the successes of the children who have been Home Educated are overlooked – without recognition or celebration.

I spent a small amount of time researching to try and find out, how long exactly, the 'apartheid Gypsy classes' were in action. I didn't get any official leads on this, and I will certainly continue my research, because information about the apartheid education of Romany-Gypsies needs to be shared far and wide. Bringing attention to this, by sharing our personal accounts will help others understand the mistrust we still hold against those in authority, regardless of the authoritarian sector they work in. Be that the police, the council, the school system, the medical sciences, care institutes or Social Services. Ethnic persecution and discrimination are rife in all.

My Grandfarver Nelson valued his children's and grandchildren's academic learning. I can remember, as clearly as if it were yesterday, his proudness of my Kathy for passing all five of the GCSE's she sat - with grade marks of As and Bs.

Grandfarver's family lines are the Smiths and Coopers. He had heard of and would have been a distant relative to Trinity Cooper - whose story I will share in the next chapter. We know, through the oral tradition of having conversations regarding who we are related to, without the need for DNA testing that the Cooper families (England wide) will all trace back to the same bloodline. It's the same for the 'Lees', 'Boswells', and 'Smiths' who also trace back to their same bloodlines (these surnames are four of the largest groups of English Romany-Gypsies).

Trinity Cooper's family, like so many other Romanies, would travel to work on farms and it was common to be settle for each of the seasons, on different farms whilst harvesting. Trinity and her family had settled in the winter opposite a ragged school, which was a charitable organization dedicated to the free education of destitute children in 19th century Britan. But even such charitable schools were not inclusive towards Romany-Gypsy children.

'The history of school desegregation for Roma' (By Margareta Matache and Simona Barbu), is an informative read which also contains an entry about our Trinity Cooper.

The 12-year-old Trinity Cooper is our very own Rosa Parks, (who was a brave and virtuous Black lady who in 1955 refused to give up her seat to a white person which led to the beginning of the American civil rights movement). Rosa is known to many people, but our Trinity Cooper is known by few. A brave young girl, who was passionate with ambition to receive an education, she applied to be instructed to school several times and was always met with repeated rejection. The reason given for denying Trinity Cooper an education within a charity school was, "In consequence of obloquy affixed" to that description of person was the grounds for her refusal. Which basically means, Romany-Gypsies, including their children were so racially despised, even the poorest of white Britons didn't want their children associating with the Gypsies. White people were strong in numbers and able to oppose the brown (olive) skinned Romany-Gypsies, and the charitable school appeased the white majority for as far as they were able to. The persistence of the Cooper family resulted in Trinity, and two of her brothers, eventually being able to access the charity school and receive an education.

Obloquy: strong public condemnation.

In my adult years, through research and meeting new people, I have come to learn that the different schools in Kent, where my family, and relatives attended, these were not isolated cases with regard to the 'apartheid education' of Romany-Gypsy pupils. Schools, and not just in the UK either, have been guilty of placing Gypsy children into isolated classrooms that did not follow the standard academic curriculum, long after Trinty Copper paved the way for Romanies to be allowed into schools.

Children were routinely placed in classrooms designed to aid pupils with special needs. Most of the time this was done without assessing if the Romany-Gypsy children had any special needs. Other times Romany-Gypsy children, as soon as they started school, were placed into a classroom that held Gypsy pupils only. This was indeed a common practice, where several of my cousins, relatives, and other people I know have also been denied a standard education, by default of their ethnicity.

The Encyclopaedia Britannica who are considered a reliable and trusted source for scholarship and literacy style stated the following (1954): The mental age of an average adult Gypsy is thought to be that of a child of ten. Gypsies have never accomplished anything of great significance in writing, painting musical composition, science, or social organisation. Quarrelsome, quick to anger or laughter, they are unthinkingly but not deliberately cruel. Loving bright colours, they are ostentatious and boastful, but lack bravery.

This Britannica assertion came just 14 years after the nazis ethnic cleansing of the Roma/Sinti/Gypsies who had been racially targeted for genocide. With the Britannica being considered such a credible source for information it is no wonder Gypsies have been continually judged as 'feeble-minded' or 'slow learners' or 'slower to move in education'; the nazis had used 'feeble-mindedness' as the reason to forcibly sterilise, hunt, murder, assassinate or to force Gypsies into labour camps way before being supposed as 'racially inferior' – rounded up, transported and imprisoned into Auschwitz (and other death camps) where uncountable lives of innocent men, women and children were ended in the gas chambers.

Further research has led me to question if there is a deliberate stratagem, which is still evident in present times in Europe, the same stratagem that was in existence up until at least the 1990s in the UK. A stratagem that is ensuring Romanies do not advance their academic abilities. I found publishments made by Amnesty International, that highlights how countries such as Greece, France, Czech Republic and Slovakia, are still segregating Romany children into seldom having a fighting chance to be educated.

I recommend the following reports:

'Segregation, bullying and fear: The stunted education of Romani children in Europe' Amnesty International, April 8, 2015, www.amnesty.org.

'Czech Republic: Systematic discrimination against Romani children in schools' Amnesty International, April 23, 2015, www.amnesty.org.

'Romani children and the right to education in Central and Eastern Europe' errc challenging Discrimination Promoting Equality,03 October 2000 www.errc.org.

'A tale of two schools Segregating Roma into special education in Slovakia' www.amnesty.org/en/wp-content/ uploads/2021/08/eur720072008eng.pdf.

We moved from Orpington to Dartford (Kent), when I was eleven, we agreed as a family not to be forthcoming regarding our ethnicity. On starting a new school our Mum wanted us placed into groups that supported our academic ability. She also wanted us to be treated the same and seen as equal to all the other pupils, and not having the security of attending a school where our own relatives would be, was a concern for our parents because this meant Kathy, and I would only have each other and worse still was that our baby sister (Sarah) was in primary completely alone. This was a worry for our Parents that in all honesty shouldn't have existed. Our Parents raised well behaved children who were sent to school to achieve the highest level of education possible, and ethnicity should never determine the level of education any child receives.

We soon made new friends in and outside of school. The next few years consisted of school days and weekend fun, like staying at my Granny-Dinkeys and Grandfarver-Nelsons. On the weekends that

THE MYSTERY IN BEING A GYPSY

we didn't stay at our Grandparents' we had our friends stay over. Mum never did mind who came to stay, and all our friends loved staying at ours. One of my friends, Victoria, who regularly stayed over at the weekends had come with us to visit my Grandparents. I had explained to her that my Grandparents lived on their own land, in a challey, not in a house. Victoria told me, "My aunt lives in a chalet on a Mobile Park Home, in Margate."

I wondered why when Gypsies live in trailers, mobile homes, or challeys the land is called a 'Site'. But when Gorgers live in mobile homes or challeys the land is called a 'Park'. I shared with Victoria that I preferred the sound of Park.

We enjoyed the day and spent most of our time playing in my Grandparents' orchard picking apples and pushing each other on our tree swing. Grandfarver took us down to his paddock, where he kept his horses, so we could feed them with a couple of the apples. Granny cooked for us and after eating, and helping with the washing up, we left to go home.

Victoria asked if she could have a sleep-over, predictably, as was common practice for my Mum she replied, "Yes, providing it's okay with your mum."

Victoria and I both knew she'd be allowed to sleep over, as she had done so many times before. There was never a time before when her mum had ever said no. Her parents went out together most Saturday nights and Victoria preferred to be at ours than stay home alone. She ran off to check with her mum and to collect her overnight bag. She was gone for quite a while, longer than was needed to go round to hers, grab an overnight bag and return. A while later she knocked at the door with a solemn look on her face and I noticed it looked as though she'd been crying. Victoria told me she wasn't allowed to stay, and I asked her, "Why?"

She flushed red and explained after telling her mum that she had the best time at my Grandparent's, who lives in a chalet and has horses, her mum had then asked whereabouts my Grandparents lived.

Maybe, as her mother that should have been a question that was worth asking 'before' she allowed her daughter to come with us!

Victoria had told her mum that my Granny lived on her own land in Kent and had announced she knew the difference between a park and a site. And there it was – 'My Mistake!' Having this conversation previously and Victoria then sharing this with her mum had disclosed our ethnicity. This was all the information that her mum needed to decide that her daughter would no longer be allowed to sleepover at ours. Worse still for Victoria, was having to tell me that her mum also said we could no longer be friends.

This is what one form of racism, among many, looks like. Two thirteen-year-old girls had a friendship that was not permitted because her parents believed that I belonged to an ethnicity that supposed me to not be good enough as a suitable friend to their daughter. To be honest, the truth is, it was my Parents who could have easily had that attitude because as far as parents went, mine didn't leave us home alone till the early hours. Mine knew where we were and who we were with. And nor have my Parents ever discriminated by skin colour, ethnicity, or creed.

4

VICIOUS RUMOURS & FEAR

August 1994: Dan and I had been courting for two years when a plot on the site, where he lived in Surrey, became available. I was apprehensive about moving and leaving my own family and friends. But Dan and I felt privileged to get a plot of our own because plots are scarce. Councils have long flouted their duties to provide sites and it's a simple case of, they have chosen 'not' to fulfill the duty. A plot (or pitch as they are also known) is a hard standing base with enough room for a trailer (caravan), mobile home, or challey (depending on which the resident owns) with an amenity block provided. An amenity block is a brick building that consists of bathroom facilities and in some they can have a small kitchen-like space. Sites can vary in size having a different number of plots per site.

On one occasion when I was in our amenity block, prepping to decorate, I was interrupted by a young woman who was around my age. Louisa, who became one of my dearest friends, will tell you a different story about the first time we met, she remembers our first meeting being at the Derby, which is held at the Epsom Downs racecourse.

This is a traditional stopping/meeting place for Romany-Gypsies, who come far and wide to attend the event. If I had to say why the Derby is such an attractive place for my people, I would tell of the teenage excitement I felt dressing up to spend the day socialising amid the funfair, with all its entrapments of the loud music and the thrills sought after from the fast and high rides. For others, it could be the market stalls or enjoying the horse racing.

The Romanies, by the time the Derby became popular, had already been regular attendees since the 'first' Epsom Derby event held on the 4th of May in 1780. So, when the Gorgers from wider society began attending the Romanies were already well established, using their unique skills as self-taught musicians to earn a living in the entertainment industry. Passed-on teachings were from parent to child which saw Romanies being able to play all types of musical instruments such as fiddles, guitars, banjos, mouth organs, accordions, and even playing the spoons - to an exceptionally high standard.

Tap dancing, for centuries has been a talent of the Romany, and long before the invention of tap shoes – Romany dancers would use a wooden flat board, with salt spread on it, to enhance the sound their feet would play. Romanies are also extremely gifted singers, and none can doubt the raw talent held to produce music that could easily rival the famously well-known composers.

Romany horse breeders would also gather at the Derby to trade their horses and the 'Gypsy Cob Vanner' breed, in my view, are the most exquisitely UK bred horses among all. It was indeed the Romany-Gypsy horse breeders who bred the Gypsy Cob Vanner into existence. The Gypsy Cobs are renowned for being dependable, having great athletic ability, intelligent, affectionate, extremely kind, and gentle whilst also being sturdy drivers. Earning a living was also done by selling flowers, practicing palmistry, fortune-telling, and boxing in the prize fighting booths. The Romanies entertaining skills were enjoyed by Royalty at the Derby long before the Gorger newcomers began to attend the races.

THE MYSTERY IN BEING A GYPSY

The above photo is my Great-Granny Liza's brother Harry Lee, 1939, at Epsom Downs. He was a well-known and extremely talented music composer and fiddle player.

For nearly half a century Romanies were a prominent part of the Derby horse race held in the Epsom Borough of Surrey. But shortly after the Gorger newcomer's arrival a vicious rumour had spread that the Gypsies were bringing an infectious disease into the Borough.

Yet, infectious disease was less likely to spread amongst Romanies because encampments were too isolated to pick up new infections and too small to contain a reservoir of old ones. Also, the very strict hygiene practises of the Romany helped to keep infections at bay. In fact, being in proximity with the newcomers would have posed more of a threat for the Romanies who could have picked up infectious diseases from the Gorgers.

Due to the baseless fear, tensions arose, and the Gorgers called for the sanction of banning all Gypsies from the Derby. During the 1930s, Romany families faced the attempts to remove them from the Downs. However, they found a champion in Lady Sybil Grant. She was the daughter of the fifth Earl of Rosebery, who had been Prime Minister in Queen Victoria's era. She was herself fond of caravanning and held a hawker's license enabling her to sell door-to-door for charity. So, she held a lot in common with the Romany-Gypsies and holding a hawking license was just one of the commonalities.

This hysteria of fear resulted in pressure being placed on the Downs Administrators. The rumour started by an 'unknown' source, had spread widely and this saw many Gorgers calling to be "Rid of the Gypsies" in a verbal witch hunt. The Downs administrators chose to appease the Gorger newcomers by banning all Romanies from the Downs. Lady Sybil again intervened and let the Romanies camp on her land. She held good relations with the Romanies getting to know them well, therefore, she had not succumbed to the hysteria of fear.

Lady Sybil's response helped the Romanies, in part, not to be viewed as a danger. But tensions remained high, and a level of hatred had grown from the fear. Many of the Gorger community already owned a generalising bias attitude toward the Romanies that they should 'all' be suspected as being petty criminals, for the crimes committed by the few with the same ethnic heritage. The Gorgers hatful and spitefully bias mindset which held accountable 'all' the

THE MYSTERY IN BEING A GYPSY

hardworking, law-abiding Romanies to be 'unjustly' viewed and hated as petty criminals, alongside their fear of Gypsies being infectious disease carriers, saw the continuation of the Gorgers protesting for the Romanies to be banned from attending the Downs.

In 1932 Lady Sybil went public in saying: "I am hoping to organize the van dwellers into a humble little Guild which will have the advantage of protecting the working Gypsies and get rid of those undesirable members who are to be found in every community."

Clearly Lady Sybil was raised with the same 'virtuous', and 'righteous' moral view, of which I was also raised to know and understand: There are good and bad in all walks of life.

Later in 1936 a local government Bill was passed, making it illegal for Romany-Gypsies to stay on the Downs, Lady Sybil then immediately responded and permitted them to stay in her field at The Sanctuary on Downs Road.

Lady Sybil wrote: "In the absence of the Gypsies, it is regretted by many persons, who consider that the Spring Meeting has lost something of its traditional character. It's considered that the racecourse yesterday looked funereal, or at the best, exceedingly dreary."

An Act of Parliament, in 1936, created the 'Epsom and Walton Downs Conservators' (EWDC) giving them the authority to run the Downs for the benefit of the public. Yet, the Romany-Gypsies who had traditionally attended the Downs since it began, and many of whom had ancestral history of living in Surrey for centuries, were not taken into consideration. When one of the first decisions made by the EWDC was to ban all Gypsies from the Downs. Lady Sybil was again vocal in expressing her views that this ban was against the Gypsies 'Rightful Heritage' as they had camped on the Downs during the Epsom Derby for hundreds of years.

The continuing conflict eventually came to a head in 1967, when summonses under the legislation for illegal camping were served on 40 Romany families. In 1969, the Downs Conservators handed the job of 'policing' over to a security company that provided 24-hour patrols to warn off campers. Disputes between the two parties continued until 1984 when another Act of Parliament was passed. Under this new law, Gypsies were finally given the right, by paying a fee to secure authorised stopping, on Epsom Downs during the Derby.

But the fear that birthed the hatred which originated from the unfounded vicious rumour still exists. 'Fear sure is the most powerfully contagious disease poisoning humanity'.

I can recall going to the Downs (Epsom Derby) that year, where Louisa remembers first meeting me, yet I have no recollection of meeting her. There was a large group of us, and we were either related, friends, or friends of friends. The teenagers who both Louisa and I hung around with were 'The Generation' of born-again Christians. Thinking of what to share next, in order, I feel will be an impossible task. So much of Louisa's and my time has been spent chatting, debating, and dreaming, that events, times, and places have over the years merged together. But this certainly won't be the last time you hear about our special relationship.

Two very special and dear friendships were formed after I first married my husband and moved to Surrey. A group of young Gorger people, around a similar age to myself, would often visit our site. They were part of a locally based church called The Generation and they used to provide a free car cleaning service as a community-building project. With their regular visits, it didn't take long to build friendships with them all.

Hayley Roberts and her family, and Russel Oliver and his family have remained our close and trusted friends to this very day. Hayley and I were expecting our first babies at the same time. When our babies were a year-old Hayley invited me to help her run a local mother and toddler's group, held at the youth center on our estate. As I am writing this, I am smiling thinking of the times we have spent together from our firstborns attending the same playgroup, to years

THE MYSTERY IN BEING A GYPSY

later when our daughters attended the same dance lessons. Also, the time we spent together when I worked for Hayley, helping to run a home-schooling project called 'The Lighthouse'. My friendship with Hayley has been, for over a quarter of a century, a very special one. She's a person I have followed by the example she leads.

Whilst on our lunch break at The Lighthouse Hayley had asked if I would answer some questions in an interview with her husband Mark for his University dissertation. She explained that Mark's study would examine the themes of influence and authority, prejudice and injustice that I had faced when petitioning local authorities to remove 'Bunds' (deliberately created surrounding banks), around the perimeter of the site where I lived.

A bund is an embankment or wall of brick, stone, concrete, or other impervious material, which forms the perimeter and floor of a compound and provides a barrier to retain liquid. Since the bund is the main part of a spill containment system, the whole system (or bunded area) is colloquially referred to as the 'bund'.

In building and planning a 'bunded area' is about keeping things from 'spilling'. So, there is a sense that the 'Gypsy site bund' was created to keep Romany-Gypsies from spilling into areas outside of the segregation (apartheid area) which the bunds provided.

Sites were created in response to the duty placed on the local authorities in law, who have in return commonly chosen to provide the 'minimum' number of individual plots needed for Romany-Gypsies and other Traveller families, living permanently within each Borough of Surrey.

I will explain in more detail, both the early development of the site and its living conditions: It was positioned at the end of the road on the furthest edge of the Borough. Being next to the river this was an area susceptible to flooding and there were no adequate sewage works. The ground was flattened, and the debris collected in this clearance, was then bulldozed to make the 'Bunds' that segregated the site.

I was informed by good authority (the councils Gypsy Liaison Officer, who held the position at the time) that this was done, "To create a pit for the Gypsies to live in".

Sites have been placed on areas of land that were unprofitable, contaminated or derelict.

Council owned sites countrywide, that were provided, are situated near either hazard zones or undesired places such as: next to rivers, motorways, under flyovers, next to railways, sewage plants, industrial estates, next to graveyards, and on waste or contaminated land. What they each have in common is that they have all been placed on the farthest edge or in the most secluded areas possible, within each of the boroughs. They were placed without any thought or consideration for health and safety. No consideration was taken that these placements could result in even more prejudice, by giving off the impression that such areas were suitable for 'Gypsy site provision' when the same areas had been commonly considered 'unsuitable' for any other building provision.

I recommend the following by Katharine Quarmby:

'Site Conditions and Health', (https:/katharinequarmby. com/2022/07/05/planning-environmental-injustice-my-findings/.

'Environmental racism, location of Traveller site and human rights, November 19, 2021, (https://katharinequarmby. com/2021/11/19/environmental-racism).

'Systemic Racism within Rigged System': New Investigation Reveals how Travellers Sites are Routinely Placed in Risky Locations, (https://bylinetimes.com/2021/05/24/systemic-racism-within-a-rigged-system-new-investigation).

The above recommendations evidence what we already know, with experiencing the structural inequalities that are levelled against us. Baroness Janet Whitaker, who co-chairs the All-Party Parliamentary Group on Gypsies and Traveller, told Byline Times: "This research exposes systemic racism within a

*planning system that is rigged against Gypsies and Travellers...
We all need somewhere to live, and a person's ethnicity should
not affect their opportunity to live in healthy surroundings."*

During the 1970s – 1990s, some local authorities were busy compulsory purchasing areas of land belonging to Romany-Gypsies.

My Grandparents' land and the surrounding plots, owned by other Romany-Gypsy families, was compulsory purchased by their local authority. The action of compulsory purchasing Romany-Gypsies' land, resulted wastefully in local authorities then providing a council site for the landowners. It's reasonable to conclude that all local authorities who obtained Romany owned lands for a pittance of the land's value under compulsory purchase orders and then provided a council site on the same land - provided nothing!

Landowners were forced to leave their land and become rent paying tenants and for those who did not accept the pittance offered, it could be argued their land was legally stolen. Also, these local authorities were falsely celebrated by Central and Local Governments for their site provision efforts.

I was given permission by George Monbiot to share his article: 'Britain's Ethnic Cleansing' - Gypsy culture is being systematically eliminated through a forced assimilation programme.

*The Romanies written about by George Monbiot, who lived
on 'Swan Farm' include my Grandparents who were one of
the families who had their land compulsory purchased.*

The article reads: Britain's Romanies always knew there was something fishy about the government's promise to let them establish their own sites, and last month the European Court confirmed it. There should, it ruled, be no special provision for Gypsies under Britain's planning laws. They would, as Robert Jones, the Minister for Planning, reaffirmed in the Guardian yesterday, have to accept the same conditions as everyone else.

Planning permission was the Gypsies' last hope. The Criminal Justice Act removed local authorities' responsibility to provide sites, and the great majority of traditional stopping places – some of which had been used by Travellers since the Bronze Age – have been barricaded during the last twenty years, which explains the record numbers of caravans now packed into official sites. Seeking permission to pitch camp on their own land, as Mr Jones advocates, is a poor substitute for wayfaring, but the only remaining means of holding their communities together.

Yet ninety per cent of all such applications are turned down. Planning, Britain's Gypsies are now coming to see, is not an opportunity but a peril, a means of forced assimilation as effective as Guatemala's integration of its Indians, or Saddam Hussein's containment of the Marsh Arabs.

For 23 years the Romanies of Swan Farm, beside the village of Ash in Kent, have tried to muddle along without permission. When, in 1973, they paid £7000 or £8000 for each plot, they knew they were taking a risk, but it had to be a better bet, they reasoned, than endless harassment by landowners and the police.

Like Gypsies almost everywhere, they were welcomed coolly by their neighbours. There were complaints of stolen cars appearing on the site and children running wild through gardens. Had Swan Farm been an ordinary housing estate, Kent County Council might have concentrated on the people who were causing the problems, but, as the settlement had no planning permission, the council was entitled to clear the whole site. At the end of May, it obtained a compulsory purchase order, and is now offering the Romanies £200-300 for their plots. Once it acquires the land, it will divide a small part of it into regular parcels, get planning permission, lay on electricity, then sell leases to the Romanies for £14,000.

The residents were astonished but found that the council has acted within the law. Without permission, the land was worth no more than its agricultural value. With permission, it acquired development zone prices.

THE MYSTERY IN BEING A GYPSY

It was ruled there should be no special provisions for Britons Gypsies but, on the same green belt land - after it had been compulsory purchased - which removed ownership of the land from the Gypsy families and transferred the ownership of the land to the council - the planning request, to overturn the greenbelt sanction, was then granted!

Continuation of the article: If they can't afford to pay all at once, the council says, they can pay in instalments, and if they can't afford that they can, like 90 per cent of Kent's Gypsies, go on the housing list.

In the meantime, a spiked fence and security lighting have been erected to keep the Romanies in. And, since a fight over the provenance of a car in May, the police have agreed to mount a 24-hour guard at the gates. With their housing situation resolved, the council enthuses, the children's schooling will be assured. The Romanies will be "empowered to have the same opportunities as other people".

It all looks neat, ordered and sensible. Admittedly, the security arrangements might appear a touch insensitive, in the light of the Gypsies' recent history. It's true, too, that without land for their horses, and with trading banned on the new site, their economic activities will come to an abrupt end, just as their community life might have some difficulty straddling the picket fences. But, newly empowered, the lucky Gypsies will now have opportunities to seek work as zero-hour contract cleaners, just like the rest of us.

The unnamed council spoke person was most definitely not on a zero-hour cleaning contract, like many of the law-abiding hard-working 'Swan Farm' landowners, that remark and the entire response from the council was nothing more than an opportunity to share snide comments.

Continuation of the article: It seems strange that we find it so hard to see what we are doing to these people. We have no such difficulty when urging Brazil to stop taking land from the Indians. China's announcement last week that it will build new schools all over Tibet to eliminate illiteracy (and a few antisocial cultural tendencies) was greeted in Britain not with delight but with repulsion. We were quick to condemn Ceaucescu for forcing Romania's Gypsies into regular housing.

Yet somehow, perhaps because the means of assimilation in Britain are so dignified, we manage to overlook them. Had our planning system been designed to exclude Travellers, it could not have been more oppressive. Strict zoning into development land (with premiums so high that only property developers need apply) and agricultural land (in which only farm buildings can be erected) leaves no room for people who need cheap plots for caravans. Their last option was not an option at all. Legally, respectably, by decent, conscientious people like the officers of Kent County Council, the Romanies and their lifestyle are being cleansed from our countryside. Our incapacity to accommodate other cultures puts the whole nation to shame. By George Monbiot, 10th October 1996, www.monbiot. com. Published in the Guardian 10th October 1996.

The age old 'all' are guilty because of the 'few' was used in this situation to compulsory purchase my Grandparents land, who for all their lives were law-abiding working-class members of society. And certainly, their children (my Mum and her siblings) were not guilty of 'running wild through the gardens'. As far back as the 1530s 'Egyptians Act', England's Romanies have been ethnically targeted having their goods and properties legally stolen.

5

INFLUENCE, AUTHORITY & UNJUST LAWS

I was triggered into making a conscious commitment to petition for the removal of the Bunds, on my site in Surrey, by a chance encounter I had with my Gorger housed neighbours. When walking to the local shop I noticed a group of women outside chatting, we exchanged smiles as I walked past. I was still relatively new to the area and thought to myself, on the way back I'd stop to have a chat with them. As I left the shops they were still outside. It was a nice day which served me with the opening line to pass pleasantries about the weather. What started out as being a friendly chat very quickly turned into an eye-opening and educational conversation, that resulted in my determination to get rid of those 'Bunds'.

One of the ladies was repeatedly looking in the direction of the site entrance whilst we were chatting. I asked if she knew anyone who lived on the site? All too soon I was subjected to listening to some truly ignorant comments being made about their beliefs regarding "Gypsy people and their behaviours". It was obvious they had not realised I lived on the site. I chose not to disclose this fact, nor to get defensive, and instead asked why they did not know any of the people living there. It had after all been a part of the council estate for three decades, predating the newer housing association buildings, which is where one of these ladies lived.

It was revealed by the women that they each held fear-based beliefs about 'those Gypsy people' who lived behind the dividing dirt-wall (Bunds). One of these women, in defending her fear of Gypsies, after I had questioned if she even knew any Gypsy people replied, "I don't know any, but when looking at the site entrance it makes me wonder what type of people need to be kept behind such an embankment."

I listened to what they each had to say and before I left that conversation, I informed the women, "You have now met a

Romany-Gypsy from the site and hopefully in doing so you will have a change of heart and opinion."

I bid them farewell as I walked away, leaving behind three embarrassed looking women. Before this, I had not understood that the Bunds had helped to create more fear being held towards us. Granted the bunds were indeed an eyesore, but my main concern had been that they were the perfect habitat for vermin, so the appearance was secondary to this. Having this conversation made me want to see through their eyes. Walking down our site entrance road I knew, that to be able to see through these women's eyes, I needed to imagine not knowing anyone who lived on the site - viewing them as strangers - and not knowing if they were good or bad people.

> *"As we all know the world is full of both regardless of ethnicity, creed, colour, gender, age, sexuality, or social class."*

It was difficult for me to pretend that I didn't know the site residents, I had lived there for nearly two years and had gotten to know them all quite well and their children would often come into my trailer, where I would help them with their homework or play games with them that incorporated subjects they struggled with in school. Our doors were always open to each other, any time in the day without appointments or dates being made.

As I walked the access road to the site I did so from a different viewpoint. I was able to take in and fully absorb the visual magnitude, and the ambiance that the dirt wall created. The disheartening feeling, I felt that day I can still recall, as I imagined how I would feel walking our access road, with its 20ft piled high mound of dirt, that also had more than its fair share of rubbish embedded in it. How would I feel if I were a Gorger who did not know anyone living on the site? The real question was, would it be fair to say I would feel anxious? The authentic truth was - I knew I would.

Our Gypsy liaison officer (GLO), Kevin Ryan had knocked on my door, as he usually did on a Wednesday. Shouting, "Come in

THE MYSTERY IN BEING A GYPSY

Kev," I'd already got up to put the kettle on. I told him that I was serious about getting the Bunds removed and that I'd had enough of waiting; many of us as the site residents had made several complaints, over the years, about the Bunds being rat infested.

I told Kevin, "I need to know who to contact directly to be taken seriously."

I was feeling that attending meetings and constantly complaining about the Bunds (due to the rat infestation), and about other site maintenance issues on our site, had only served as a talking shop. I was seeing no action taking place. I had previously, on several occasions, shared with council meeting attendees the reasons the Bunds should be removed. I always complained and asked for help from any professional who attended.

I had been promised so many times by the people who attended these local authority meetings, that they would "look into this for me" that I eventually lost faith in their verbal promises. A considerable amount of time had passed without any advice or assistance materialising. No one was seemingly able to point me in the right direction to find out who was the person I needed to speak with. I just wanted to find out who was the right person or people who could help, but all I had encountered were those who couldn't. The world had long passed the days when verbal communication, with the Council's Gypsy Liaison Officer could bring about a solution to site maintenance issues.

Daisy (my mother-in-law) has lived on our site for over 35 years and was actively involved in petitioning the local council to provide rubbish collection for the 16 plots (16 families). A system of providing skips and replacing them fortnightly had been in place for years, from when the site first opened. This was a common practice on most local authority sites. Site residents pay council tax, rent, water, and electricity just the same as everyone else, but they were not provided with the same rights to receive the services. The council contracted road sweepers do not come on to any of the sites that I know of.

4 9

Also, the council contractors who cut the grass and litter-pick on the surrounding council-owned lands (around the houses), do not maintain the surrounding area of the sites. The same excuse is given to anyone complaining: No-one knows who owns the land, and therefore nobody is aware of who is responsible for maintaining the site entrance or the surrounding areas.

Back in the day, when all people were much more engaged verbally, my mother-in-law had collected signatures from of all the site residents, and then handed over the petition to their Gypsy Liaison Officer who held the position in 1985. Concerningly, the system in place; whereby all household rubbish (including food waste) was thrown into a skip had served to attract the wildlife. Especially, the long tails (rats) who would visit and hang out around the site, uninvited by the residents.

This problem was created by those in authority, who are widely considered as 'intelligent' professionals. This decision to have an open rubbish skip certainly helped to feed the bigoted biased mindsets of racists and those that discriminate against us, as such people would certainly not care to understand the reason behind the accumulation of vermin, choosing instead to view the potential health risk to residents, (for example of contracting Weil's disease which is carried and spread by several animals including rats), as a 'Gypsy Problem'.

Those who thought up and authorised this system of waste disposal were either complete dinlows (fools) or they simply didn't care what potential health risks they could be creating for the residents. In addition, previous methods of council tax and rent charges for the site, were, in my view, an extortionate rip-off when taking into consideration sites were excluded from rubbish collection, grass cutting, litter picking and road sweeping. The council used, and some councils still do use, the monies collected from rent charges to pay for site maintenance and up-keep, (but that's only on the sites where the residents are fortunate).

Mostly sites have been allowed to become rack to ruin due to decades of no maintenance at all, and the shoddy workman ship of creating 'pits for the Gypsies to live in' meant very few sites

THE MYSTERY IN BEING A GYPSY

originally provided adequate and safe provisions, in the first place. Site residents rent money, could have paid for an adequate sewage system. But instead, a portion of the rent money was being used to pay a private contractor to cut the grass, litter pick and road sweep (not forgetting the skip system: how much money was wasted paying for large skips that was collected and then replaced fortnightly for years instead of the regular waste collection as elsewhere in the Borough).

When I discovered that our site had a private contract with a company to sweep the site road, on a 'when needed basis', I made a very strong suggestion that our rent money paying for this contract should stop being wasted with immediate effect. Because we, the site residents, collectively swept the road once a month ourselves. Therefore, a private company was being paid for years, for doing nothing. This was a complete waste of money, and I would be surprised to learn if the Government audit office, which is supposed to check on how money is used by local authorities, do so when its money collected from site residents and allocated for site maintenance.

Contrary to popular belief - that we don't pay rates - I would argue all tenants on council sites have been made to pay double.

Kevin, (the GLO) despite his best efforts wasn't having much luck with getting our site maintenance issues resolved. It was preferred by the local authority to pay out money on a regular annual basis to keep the outdated cesspit sewage system going. The cost to renew the sewage system was considered 'too much money to spend on the site'.

Continuously when the cesspit is full, or the pump once again breaks down, the smell would be enough to make anyone vomit. Imagine using your bathroom sink to brush your teeth in the morning, and upon turning on your tap the stench of raw sewage is what greets you. I cannot help but wonder if dog walkers or those who enjoy the nature walk, that runs behind our site, would believe the stench is due to the 'dirty Gypsies'.

Even Kevin wasn't sure if responsibility of maintenance was that of the County Council or our local Borough because the site was, back then, owned by the County but run by local Borough. Our family friend Russel had advised me to communicate all site issues, concerns, and complaints in writing so that there would be a paper trail. I asked Kevin if he would proofread my letter and he said he would be happy to. So, I wrote complaining about the Bunds (the dividing-dirt-wall) including all the other site maintenance issues. This was the first time in my life that I had found myself needing to write a formal complaint.

I listed every possible reason I could think of to get the council to remove the Bunds. From the fact that they were rat-infested, (due to being the perfect habitat for longtails), to the dangers of falling clumps of mud, rubbish, and debris after heavy rains. After months of attending meetings to no avail, a few weeks after writing the letters and sending them to the relevant different departments within the council (as advised by our family friend Russel), I began to find the people that no one from the meetings had allegedly been unable to find. Suddenly, the wheels were turning in the right direction.

I believed I'd finally received a stroke of luck after spending so long without finding the wheel in the first place. I didn't get my desired hope of the council removing the dividing-dirt-wall completely, but they did considerably reduce the height of it. They rounded the tops off, seeded the banks and planted laurel bushes on top. They then took out a regular contract to manage the longtails (happily paid for out of our rent payments). I was pleased with the outcome and after the works were carried out it looked like a more welcoming place to the people living 'outside' the dirt wall.

Whilst I was at my Gorger friends, in Hayley's and Marks home, answering Marks questions about the process I went through, providing this information to support his dissertation, they shared with me that for them, as local teenagers, it was almost a dare to venture beyond the dirt wall of the site entrance. Considering this dividing dirt-wall was approximately 20 ft high x 300 ft in length, their eyes offered no help to see beyond it. It would take for them to bravely walk the access road to be able to see the site, to know who and what lays behind the wall. They faced the fear of the unknown.

I will now explain why local authorities were placed with duties to provide sites. What I do not have any clue about though, is why (before the 2004 Housing Act) they were given the choice to provide between a minimum and maximum number – instead of the number of plots needed which led to 'undersupply'.

In 1960, The Caravan Sites (Control of Development) Act in England stopped almost all new private sites from being built until 1972 (this took away the rights for Romany-Gypsies to provide for themselves). This Act was legislation that allowed for mass evictions and harassment of Gypsies across the country. The new law required the occupiers of land to gain a license from the council before it could be used to live on. Many historical stopping places or land owned by Romany-Gypsies were immediately determined illegal to stay on (which created more nomadism). This law included living seasonally on farmland, for work, and stopping on common land was also made illegal, you know that land that once existed that 'we' members of the public owned as a collective?

I recommend:
'Foundation for common land. A Guide to Common Land and Commoning', (https://foundationforcommonland.org. uk/a-guide-to-common-land-and-commoning;).

The law now required a site license had to be obtained for people to peacefully stop. Equally, with significant prejudice still existing among councils and local communities objecting to applications, obtaining a site license was near impossible in most cases. Eviction and harassment of Gypsies and Travellers reached a crisis point and it was common practice to see on the TV news, Romany people and other Travellers being forcibly removed by the police from their own land, from roadsides or common lands.

Under Section 23 of this 1960 Act, local authorities were given the power to close the commons to Travellers. In Section 24 it is written there is a power which enables councils 'to open caravan sites' to compensate for the closure of the commons. Section 24 was an essential compensation because without anywhere to stop legally Gypsies and Travellers would be forced to travel without ceasing!

This Act was passed in Parliament, under the Conservative prime minister - Harold Macmillan, and made staying anywhere, on any land that did not have a council licence, a crime overnight. Harold Macmillan's time in office ran from 1957 – 1963. Macmillan, the 1st Earl of Stockton was known for his pragmatism and in this Act his Parliament were perhaps trying to strike some sort of balance so that it would be passed without too much challenge.

Even though the compensation to provide sites was written into this Act; County and Borough councils had legally been given a choice of how many plots to provide on each of the sites, (maybe this was due to what's known as a loophole, which had conveniently provided local authorities with a choice).

An Act of Parliament creates a new law or changes an existing law. An Act is a Bill (first stage of passing legislation) that is approved by the House of Lords, and the House of Commons, and has been given Royal Assent by the Monarch before passing into law. I am acquainted with many different local authority and county council owned sites in both Kent and Surrey. I lived on a site in Gravesend (Kent) with my parents for two years, in 1990 before they moved back into housing. This site is situated next to a sewage plant and the smell was an actual aggravated assault on the nostrils. Sometimes the smell was so unbearable it could make me physically throw up.

The site I live on now in Surrey is indeed cramped and I do feel this area is far too small, even for the minimum number of 16 family's (16 plots). Fire safety distancing is said to be okay by the council officials, who then go on to inform us that the local

THE MYSTERY IN BEING A GYPSY

fire inspector agrees. But in comparison to other sites, ours isn't a bad one.

A family living on our site had an electrical fire a few years ago. It was terrifying for us all. It was devastating for the family, who lost their home and everything in it. I may add it's virtually impossible to get insurance if you live on a council-owned site and indeed this was the case for this family who'd just lost everything. They had no home or contents insurance. Their next-door neighbours' home also caught on fire. I am not able to comprehend how many of the sites, that crammed either the minimum or maximum number of plots (families) onto them can possibly meet standard fire regulations for the safety of residents.

If I am going to be honest, I do not believe that they do. Indeed, it seems to be a very different case, regarding fire safety standards, when it comes to the 'privately-owned' mobile home parks. I was standing with the mother, whose home had just burned down to the ground, when the fire brigade finally arrived, 20 minutes later, after several calls had been made. The water supply held on the fire engine that arrived first was used very quickly. To our horror we discovered, when the firefighters tried to tap into the main water supply which is located on the site, in car park, that the connector was corroded. It was impossible to even open it, least of all connect to it. Unless you have witnessed a site firer you may not be able to fully comprehend the dangers imposed to all site residents.

The challeys, mobile homes and trailers energy supplies are either oil or gas. But not in the same way gas is supplied into houses, our gas is supplied by gas cylinders (gas bottles). Imagine the outcry if a flat or house caught fire and the fire brigade couldn't connect to the nearest water supply, even without the added risk to tenants because of gas bottles and oil tanks.

After the fire, I went through a lengthy process, assisted by our Gorger friends Hayley, Mark and Russel, in alerting all relevant bodies to our fire safety concerns. Despite this, absolutely nothing materialised from doing so. The site still does not have a single fire safety measure in place. I have yet to visit a council owned site that meets the fire safety standards which are required, by law, on private mobile home sites. Actually, I have yet to visit a council site that has 'any' fire safety regulations.

On privately owned sites relating to fire safety, Section 5(3A) of the 1960 Act lays down many procedures for license holders to follow and maintain. Yet, sites that are owned and maintained by local authority do not have to adhere to any of the fire safety regulations.

When Hayley and Mark were laughing about their experiences of how it felt for them to venture onto our site, back in the day, they told me they had felt like naughty teenagers who were about to do something they shouldn't. They were each daring the other, from their group, to see who would take the lead and walk onto the site first. They were nervous about what the people would be like who lived 'inside' the dividing-dirt-wall. Hayley told me how our friend Russel led their group onto the site of the unknown.

Listening to my friends laughing whilst sharing their stories about having to "get their braves up" to come onto the site where I lived, posed to be an uncomfortable listen for me. Even though a decade in time had passed from petitioning the authorities to remove the Bunds, old negative feelings arose with fresh new ones layered on top. To learn that my friends also felt afraid of the unknown people being kept behind the dividing-dirt-wall, it felt dejecting.

Those in authority, who were involved in making the decisions for site provision have evidenced just another reason for us to have a lack of trust and respect for those in positions of influence and power of decision making. They chose the land areas and provided the bare minimum of plots on each of the sites. The majority of council provided sites were placed on contaminated ground or near dangerous areas. Yet, the residents who moved onto such sites did not know, and most still don't have any idea, that they are living on contaminated land.

THE MYSTERY IN BEING A GYPSY

But those decision-makers, who were in authority at the time, they surely knew? I wonder how many illnesses and premature deaths could be attributed to living on contaminated wasteland?

Was it the authoritarians' added bigoted bias attached, that allowed them to not care? The attitude of those involved in making the decisions was to, "Just create a pit for the Gypsies to live in". And that still stings.

6

THE PEN IS MIGHTIER THAN THE SWORD

I understood much later that writing the letters is what set the wheel in motion. My Dad would often use the phrase, "The pen is mightier than the sword." I would come to learn, through life experience, that indeed it is.

Kevin, (our GLO) was a great help to me and when proofreading my letters, he made suggestions on how to use professional language; a language that did not exist within my vocabulary. He became my very own private tutor, and due to Kevin's invitation, I began to regularly attend meetings held by the local Traveller Liaison Group (TLG).

The TLG holds a 'multi-agency' meeting which takes place at the Town Hall, which is the centre of local government authority in the Borough. They are professional gatherings, of agencies whose services are targeted at the minority (excluded) group. The services are represented by: Gypsy Liaison Officer, a solicitor, housing services, environmental health, health visitor, district nurse, primary care agencies, community dental services, social workers, intercultural and language services, the curriculum manager for family literature and adult reading and police-community safety officers.

The meetings focus is on council-owned Gypsy sites, and more importantly the people occupying them. They had been in existence without our knowledge. None of us, as the site tenants, knew there were meetings being held where discussions and decision making takes place on our behalf – prior to Kevins invite.

Kevin shared with me that he didn't understand why such meetings took place without any Romany-Gypsy representation. He said, "You would be a great contribution to these meetings, and I would appreciate it if you came along."

After taking a bit of time to think about it, I agreed to attend. It was all very formal and like nothing I had personally experienced

THE MYSTERY IN BEING A GYPSY

before. When we arrived at the Town Hall I had to sign in and I was then given an identity lanyard to wear around my neck, which permitted my entry into the building, to a place that wasn't accessible to the general members of the public. I felt nervous about attending the meeting and that stemmed from a fear of the unknown. It's human nature to fear that of which we do not know. Feeling this fear served to make me even more determined to see the removal of the dividing-dirt-wall, because the 'Bunds' alone had created fears for the Gorgers who lived out-side the dividing-dirt wall. I was hoping the TLG meeting would be the perfect opportunity to raise the site maintenance issues and request the removal of the Bunds.

I promised myself that my nerves (feeling uncomfortable) would not get the better of me, and depending on the agenda of the meeting, if the opportunity to speak arose then I would do so. Kevin led us to a conference room where there was a drinks machine available, at no cost, to the attendees. I got myself a latte and Kevin a cup of green tea. We took our seats around a large oval wooden table. Formal introductions were another first for me and I was pleased when Kevin introduced himself and followed on by sharing my name announcing me as a colleague. Which saved me from having to introduce myself.

Formal Introductions still feel awkward for me, even though since my first TLG meeting I have gone on to attend many different multi-agency meetings. All my life I had only ever needed to introduce myself in relation to whose daughter I am (I'm Perrin and Betsy's girl). Within my own ethnic community, when meeting someone new for the first time, its customary to speak about who our parents and grandparents are, as well as sharing our family surnames. In doing so another English Gypsy will know someone from my family personally or at least know of them.

An enthusiastic woman kicked off the meeting by sharing with us that she had won a small 'Pot of Gold'. This meant she had

59

acquired funding that could be used for a Gypsy project. She believed her idea of how to spend this money was a fantastic one. I listened to her sharing with us that she wanted to hire a bus to go onto all the sites in Surrey which would then provide dental hygiene lessons for the children. I was astounded at what I was hearing. However, I had promised myself I would only speak about site maintenance especially because this was my first meeting and I went into this meeting with myself made and agreed mental contract to listen, and more importantly to learn.

Russel had asked me a question many years ago that has always stuck in my mind, it has served to remind me, many times since, to listen to learn. The question, "Would you prefer to be a big fish in a small pond or a small fish in a big pond?" was one that I needed no time to think about to give my answer, "I would prefer to be a small fish in the ocean."

And as my Granny-Dinkey would say, "We have two ears to listen and one mouth to speak, we should listen twice as much as we talk!"

The enthusiastic lady asked, "Does anyone have any questions?"

I automatically responded, "I am interested to learn if anyone here has had a filling or any other dental treatment due to suffering from tooth decay?"

Everyone indicated that they had received such treatment by either nodding or saying, "They'd had a filling or even several fillings."

I shared with the attendees that I have never had a filling. I then told them the reason I wanted to know about their own dental treatment received, was to highlight that dental hygiene wasn't only a 'Gypsy problem'. I went on to say, "I am a Romany-Gypsy, and I have never needed dental hygiene treatment."

Quite early in the meeting, the attendees then learned that my interest in being involved was indeed an ethnic one.

I shared that I believed I could suggest a more beneficial way for the funding to be spent. I was then bombarded with niceties and questions:

THE MYSTERY IN BEING A GYPSY

"So lovely to have you join us."

"Do you live on a site, in a caravan?"

"Do you have a wagon?"

"How would you like to see this money spent?"

I suggested the bus could instead be a library bus, as I felt it would be a wonderful way to introduce books to pre-school children. Without facing any opposition, it was agreed as an alternative to the dental hygiene bus.

I had a feeling that besides the health visitor, social worker, and Kevin, that the other TLG attendees had never knowingly met a person of my ethnicity before. It seemed for one-half of them it was a treat to meet an ethnic Romany-Gypsy, and the other half, they looked a little disgruntled. My observations of their facial expressions, body language and lack of interest in engaging with me told me so.

I had deliberately opened a dialog that resulted in the TLG attendees to disclose information about their dental hygiene to highlight the fact, many people regardless of ethnicity, creed or colour have a lack of hygiene skills, and I may add - it's not just dental hygiene either.

We had a short comfort break and walking back towards the meeting room, I was met with an embarrassed-looking Kevin who informed me, that my presence at the meeting was problematic for some of the other attendees. I was not informed 'who' from the attendees felt my attendance was 'problematic' because Kevin did not share this information with me; even though I did ask. However, he did tell me that some were uncomfortable because they had never held a meeting about Gypsy matters (such as site maintenance, education, health, and projects), with a member of the Gypsy community present!

It had been agreed by the attendees when I had left the room, that Kevin (who knew me personally) would be the one to inform me that I had to leave once the first half of the meeting had finished. The 'official' reason given, when Kevin and I returned to the meeting room, was announced by the Chair that there was a family living on one of the Surrey sites, whose situation was going to be discussed by the professionals. I obviously didn't believe this reason because of what Kevin had already told me (some were uncomfortable discussing Gypsy matters with a Gypsy present). I responded directly to the Chair, "I believe my input may be valuable, because no one from this family being discussed are present to speak for themselves."

I had automatically assumed that the discussions which was going to take place in the second half of the meeting, would be regarding some sort of plot issue on a site. I was then informed, again by the Chair, the family in question had children and their risk assessments would be spoken about. Due to confidentiality risks, I'd be asked to leave. Given this information I had a change of heart and completely agreed, I should not be present for the second half.

I absolutely understood the importance to the duty of care to protect vulnerable children and I felt an overwhelming need to assert that confidentiality should be held with high regard by us all. As such I took the opportunity to ask the Chair, "Who else will not be permitted to stay for the second half due to confidentiality risks?"

I felt just as strongly that only the qualified professionals, who had received safeguard training, should be able to attend the second half, as they felt about me not being present.

There was some incredibly nervous twitching and seat repositioning once I had asked, what I believed to be a perfectly plausible question. Kevin then replied, "I will also be leaving the second half of the meeting, we arrived together, and we will leave together."

I appreciated Kevin's loyalty, but I wanted to understand how meetings that involved potential venerable children, were conducted, when those children were Gypsies.

I knew for sure that confidential issues, such as safeguarding children, should not be discussed in the presents of all the attendees present; some of whom were from the housing services, environmental health, community dental services, intercultural and language services, curriculum manager for family literature and adult reading, as well as

THE MYSTERY IN BEING A GYPSY

the Gypsy Liaison Officer: none of whom had formal safeguarding roles. I was certain that for them to be present it was a total breach of confidentiality protocols just as it would have been for me to stay.

I stated, "I had assumed the topic of discussion, about this family, would be in relation to a site matter. If there is a child safeguarding concern, why isn't it a Social Services matter opposed to a TLG meeting one?"

After a period of silence and some of the council committee members shooting each other wide-eyed looks, I was informed that the second half of the meeting would continue with the Chair, health visitor, and the social worker present. The other attendees were going to leave alongside Kevin and me.

This first meeting I attended shaped all the future TLG meetings, where I was never again asked to leave due to confidential concerns being discussed. I should have made an official complaint against the TLG but as a younger woman, I was pleased to win the battle. But with hindsight I should have gone all out to win the war. Those in authority who were responsible for allowing vulnerable families with children to be discussed in the presence of unqualified TLG meeting attendees would have deserved their reprimanding had I gone on to make a formal complaint; something which I regret not doing to this present day.

Later, Kevin had confirmed there were indeed attendees present, who regularly get together to discuss and make choices on behalf of Romany-Gypsies but who had never knowingly met any (the probability is that most people have indeed met a Romany-Gypsy, but they don't know that they have because it wasn't disclosed). Kevin shared this information with me, when I had gone to collect a computer, Phil (Kevins wife) had given me because they had gotten a new one and had kindly gifted me their old one. I then had access to the internet and fell in love with learning all over again. I started researching and found out that Romany people were known by many different names, depending on which country they lived in. I found it all so fascinating, to be learning there was this written history about my ethnic group.

I discovered how popular it is to call all Gypsies 'Roma'. However, the word Roma is only inclusive of the Roma themselves. I learned by surfing the web that there are Roma and other Romany people who regard the word 'Gypsy' to be a racial slur. But this is not true it is an alteration of Gypcian, a worn-down Middle English dialect from Egypcien 'Eyyptian'. Most English Romany-Gypsies (Romanichal), know our ancestors said they had come from a land called 'Little Egypt' which was the name given to part of Peloponnese peninsula in what is now Greece. We have been taught this by our own ancestors, it wasn't the Gorger who assumed our land of origin due to the darkness of skin.

Let's face it, Gypsy is the international word - correctly or incorrectly – that is used and recognised for all Romany people. Gypsy describes the Romanichal, Welsh Kale, Sinti, Gitanos, and Manouche, to name but a few. However, I would never ethnically label any person because all have the rights to have the term, they prefer, used and respected.

I had learned quite a lot about other cultures, ethnicities, histories, and religions in school but nothing, not a single thing about my own ethnic group. I came to learn ours is a sad history that's been dominated by racism, hatred, persecution, slavery, and murder. With blurred vision from the tears welling up in my eyes, at some of the horrors I read, I'd continue to read until the early hours of the morning. I couldn't get enough. It was like I had a thirst for discovering everything I could about the Romany people, my people and yet at the same time, no matter how much I found out - the good, the bad and the extremely ugly - I couldn't quench the thirst.

When I'd visit my parents, or they'd visit us, at some point, the subject would turn to 'Romany history from around the world'. Neither of my parents were as shocked as I was about the terrible, disgusting, and inhumane treatment that Romanies have endured. Dad only ever had one question, "Why are Romany people throughout the world hated and despised so much?"

My Dad wanted me to see if I could find out what the Romany people did wrong, what were they guilty of, what did they do that was so evil that we are disliked and discriminated against, by the vast majority worldwide, still to this present day. My interest became an obsession, as I tried to find the answer to my Father's question.

My Dad's sudden and unexpected death, on the 1st of June 2011 was such a shock to me and my family. We all suffered for the most part in silence. I understand now a little better how the mind and the body work. If any of us should find ourselves first at the scene of a car accident, where there's two passengers, one is screaming and crying, and the other is quiet and still, it's the quiet one we should attend to first because they are suffering the most and their body has gone into shock.

The loss of my father who was 57 had left us all feeling numb with shock. It took over a year for me to begin to come to terms with the fact that I'd never again, in my lifetime, see my Dad. I had feelings of confusion and to say I was suffering a low ebb would be an understatement. The grieving process is difficult for anyone but just like so many things we each go through in life; we have no choice but to learn how to live on.

Living on a site I was surrounded by people, but the fact is others were of no comfort to me. I spent many days, weeks, and months alone in my own home whilst my children were at school and my husband was at work. I did the only thing I knew how to do to cope with the loss of losing my Dad. I'd sit, pull up my knees to my chest, and fold my arms around my legs, I'd lay my head on my knees and the fact that I was self-comforting made me miss and yearn for my Dad even more.

I didn't cry, I couldn't. I wasn't in touch with my own emotions. I just felt empty and lost. I cried only once during the first year of losing my Dad. It was when Russel knocked at my door with flowers and chocolates. He said, "I won't stay, I just wanted to pop down to let you know we are thinking about you and praying for you and the family buddy."

Russel handed me the sympathy gifts and said, "I'll leave you to have some time."

That one act of kindness and thought shown, had left me on my knees crying behind the door I just closed after he left. You see my Dad was the type of person who would want to check in on someone but at the same time, he would not impose. He was the person, above all others, who I could easily confide in. His was the opinion I both trusted and valued. My Father was the most gentle and non-selfish person I have ever known, he has never let me down.

The second time I cried was when I was standing alone in my bedroom, on the first anniversary of my Dad's death. I was feeling totally engulfed by the empty loneliness inside of me. It's so difficult to explain the impact his loss has had on me and the sheer scale of despair I was feeling, which was because on that day I'd come out of the shock and numbness facing the fact he was no longer here. I gave in to the reality that in my life left on this earth I would never again cuddle or be cuddled by my Dad. I cried out loud in response to the pain I felt inside. I spoke, not in my mind but out loud, "Dad do you know it all now?"

I heard the tremble in my own voice, I was in desperation, contemplating life, and the existence of continuation after death.

My Father and I would discuss the endless possibilities of who and what God may, or may not be, for hours with no end. I was drowning in my thoughts and emotions that were far too big for me to control. I can only describe the physical pain in an analogy of being a field mouse when the boa constrictor crushes all evidence of oxygen from its body. I've heard it said so many times how the heart really does ache, and this is true but also the entire body is crushed and left lifeless by an invisible force constricting the air we breathe. I suddenly became aware of the grief-anxiety that I had lived with for so long – I had no conscious awareness that a whole year had slipped by, as I had barely noticed, but I was sure I still needed my Dad.

I had called out to God many times before, on numerous occasions, whilst driving down to my family in Kent. Alone in the car, I'd find myself letting out a scream filled with hurt and anger towards God; the God source, the universe, the higher energy, the creator (it doesn't make an ounce of difference 'to me' the name for the source that's supposed to be responsible for it all). All the hurt, the pain, loneliness, emptiness, and despair I'd scream it out and get lost in those moments, completely void of time.

Eventually the soreness from the pain felt in my throat from screaming would snap me back into reality.

On this day in my room when I called out, there was no anger left inside me. It had all gone; time had managed to burn it out. I called to my Dad, with the same desperation as I had called out to God many times previously, "Dad do you know it all now?" In an instant a warm peace fell over me. I couldn't feel my physical self, not the ground beneath my feet nor the weight of my own body. I couldn't hazard a guess just how long this 'warmth of peace and pure love' had lasted. I stood drenched in the most beautiful feeling I've ever felt. There was no noise that I could hear, (and that's strange living on a cramped site) there was only the most pleasant warmth that surrounded me, every single inch of my being could feel this energy. In response to feeling this energy of pure love I whispered, "I understand, I love you."

I'd received my confirmation that there's more to us all than this experience of life. At that moment, nothing else existed but the feeling that held me. It was a feeling I felt both inside and outside at the same time, it was the most pleasant perfect peace. The sense of calm and the overwhelming love was so real and powerfully strong. I can honestly say I have never again, nor had I ever before, experienced anything like it. I have since read other people's experiences of feeling this "perfect peace wrapped up in the warmth of pure love" and that was when I read a book, about five years after I had my own experience. The book was about those who believe they have had Near Death Experiences.

7

A STEP BACK IN TIME

When I was fifteen, I gave my heart to God and believed my place in heaven was secured, by accepting Jesus as my Lord and Saviour. I had developed a fascination with the Bible's writings, from being a small child who attended Sunday school. And from listening to my Grandfarver-Nelson question and debate the Bible's writings with his Christian friend Ricky from being 9 years of age. This furthered the fascination that would see me studying to learn everything I could about the Bible, and the Bible's history.

I have also spent many hours researching different religions and faith beliefs after deciding to know more than what is written in the Bible. Which helped to serve me in finding my own spiritual peace. I learned about the ancient beliefs of my own ethnic group. Which are centered around love and peace, and I truly believe when acting from a place of love no one can go far wrong in this lifetime. Love unites all people living on this planet, no matter their creed, skin colour, race, ethnicity, age, gender, sexuality, or social class. There is only the opposite of love, which is hate, and that is the good and bad that can be found within us all.

The older generations of Romany have long held a belief of their own that it's mogadi to be spiritually unclean. Viewing religions that have used their writings to promote theft of land, slavery, ownership of women, murder, and being the chosen ones who wield the power that enslaves others, as evil.

Around the same time of finding my own spiritual peace, my friend Louisa had not long arrived back from Holland. She had seen refugee, women, men, and children walking alongside a motorway with nowhere to call home, carrying their only possessions with

THE MYSTERY IN BEING A GYPSY

them. It had brought her to tears because she had empathy and it pained her heart thinking of their lives, especially the children. Louisa and I have long felt the need to help people who are less fortunate than ourselves.

This desire to help has been with us both from being teenagers and together we have regularly raised money to donate to the homeless, or children's hospitals or taking part in the food bank challenge, that we started via Facebook in 2015. We have grown up listening to our grandparent's generation tell us how generous and kind they all were to each other. Culturally we have always been a very charitable ethnic group. With Louisa and me, our similarities and passion to help others, has, over the years, cemented our friendship to be an unbreakable one.

I would listen to my Granny reminiscing about the good old days, and many people of her generation would say the same thing, "They had it hard, but they all helped each other out."

My Granny would hawk with groups of other women. They'd go out calling, to earn money helping to keep their own families. Selling anything from flowers to lucky heather (the belief in the power of good energy isn't in the heather itself; it is believed, the power is in projecting good energy (prosperity) onto others). Some of the men would also sell from door-to-door: either their grafting services, selling logs or provide knife grinding services (sharpening objects from kitchen knives to garden shears).

The older people would tell us about their good and hard days out hawking. Their money earned kept the food tables going for many. My Granny-Dinkey told me, "On the hard days when her relatives, friends or neighbours didn't manage to sell out, all the women would help each other and walk the streets to knock the doors, or call the shops, until everyone in their group had enough grub money," (money for food shopping).

The days they all had it hard, and there were many of those, it would be a case of throwing any vegetables and meat they had into one big pot and whoever was there when it was cooked would be fed. I listened to my Granny telling me about the police (*bori sherro muskra mushes*) who were in the habit of visiting their stopping places, to tell them they had to move on and how they'd make sure to kick over their cooking pots before they left. I'd be drawn in listening intently to these stories because Granny-Dinkeys sorrowful eyes didn't need to shed tears, to show me the misery this caused them. It was a common practice for the police to kick over pots of food and this was done to many and any Romany families who the police came across.

Contrary to the romanticisation stories that have been told, of the Gypsies living in the woods, who owned free and wild spirits, living a trouble and carefree life, dancing around a firer; the truth is, living in the woods was for no other reason than to hide away from persecution! My Gran said, "It didn't matter if they were your family, relatives, friends, or just another family pulled up who you didn't even know, whoever was there they'd be fed. If you didn't have enough to go around, then the adults would go without to make sure all the children were fed – so long as the borlows hadn't visited!"

My Granny-Dinkey was a good old caller and a hard-working woman. She would often return with clothes, shoes, and bedding. There was an older woman stopping near her, called Aunt Annie. This lady was on the larger size and when my granny returned with clothes she would shout over to her, "Any big sizes in there for me my skinner?" (One of my Granny's nicknames, Dinkey was also her nickname. Rose-Tilly is my Granny's name, but I never heard anyone call her by it).

My Gran talked highly of all Aunt Annie's family; my Granny-Dinkey was a godmother to Aunt Annies youngest son.

My Grandfarver-Nelson was also best friends with Aunt Annie's eldest son, they were all extremely close being raised together. Coincidently Aunt Annie's second son Benny (Bert) is my husband's grandfather. It's a small world!

My Grandfarver-Nelson died of cancer at the age of 59, when I was 15, so, I loved nothing better than listening to Bert reminisce about the 'good old days' as his stories gave me a version of my Grandfarver, that I didn't know. They had some good times being young, carefree, and single. They also knew hard times being young fathers, in their early twenties during a time it was hard for everyone, as this country was still recovering after WW2 at the start of the 1950s.

Granny-Dinkey was a child and young teenager during the war. I would listen to her tell me stories about what she would call 'Having a Laugh'. Granny's parents, relatives and other Romanies stopped on waste ground during the war, next to a gas station in corks meadow pit, in Kent. Because it's always been about 'safety first' when it comes to decisions made by authorities regarding Romany-Gypsies. Obviously, that's my sarcasm: because strangely enough, they were permitted to stay on the gas pit, without harassment from the police for decades.

Above is a photo my Granny was given; her family was staying on this gasworks site during the war and my Mum was born here, a decade later in a wagon, in 1954.

Granny told me that during the war, she and the other children would light a candle inside a jar and run around the gas pit singing, "Jack, Jack show your light."

Adults from all directions would swing open their doors and shout, "Blow the candle out you divvy little children, you're gonna get the lot of us blown up."

My Granny-Dinkey would laugh heartily at this memory, she could clearly see the danger that during a blackout, living next to a gas station; to be running around shining a light was a deadly game. What was funny to her as an old lady was thinking about how brazen she was to be doing such a thing time and time again. Whilst still laughing she'd say, "They should have got hold of us and beat us rotten."

After laughing so heartily (and I'd be laughing alongside her), she would draw in a long breath. Just as soon as she did, a sorrowful look would fall over her face and she'd say, "They were hoping we'd all get blown up in one hit ya-no, they were hard old times my Genta it was a worrying time, even though I was a child, and I didn't know it all. But I knew about my father leaving to fight in the war, I remember being trashed to death then. Me dad pulled us down Bournemouth, before he went off to fight, to a stopping place down there that wasn't next to gas works."

Above photo: My Granny-Dinkeys Father: James Baker 24th August 1907- 4th January 1970.

THE MYSTERY IN BEING A GYPSY

We lost my Granny Dinkey in 2019, she needed end-of-life care and was cared for, in her own home. In the last few months of her life, carers and the district nurse needed to visit. I would stay the weekends down at my Granny's to give my Mum some respite and took pleasure in taking a turn to help care for my Gran. One of these weekends when her carers had arrived, Mum told them they were not needed this morning because Granny's needs had been taken care of and she was sleeping. The two carers (who I will call Diane and Lorraine) had become quite fond of both my Mum and my Granny. Mum offered them in for a cup of tea.

After months of knowing these carers, Mums tea break invite had served us in discovering the reason why they didn't have any prejudice and were comfortable with coming onto the Gypsy site where my Granny lived. Diane shared with us that her grandparents (on her mother's side) are Romany. Mum asked who she was one of (related to) and we found out she was related to Granny-Dinkeys people, through our family line of the Johnsons. Mum and Diane worked out that she was the granddaughter of my Granny's second cousin.

We learned Diane had worked as a carer for 12 years, but her employee and colleagues did not know her ethnic heritage. My Granny's newfound relative had confirmed, what Mum and I already believed we knew: None of the other carers wanted to provide care for my Granny because they held biases toward Gypsies.

Before they left, Diane spoke directly with her colleague asking, "Can you not disclose, to any of our other colleagues, what we have just spoken about?"

And she seemed reassured with the response from Lorraine who promised she wouldn't.

Diane didn't want the other carers to know we'd just found out that she is related to our family because she was concerned about facing institutionalised racism. It was no surprise to hear racism and prejudice against Romany-Gypsies was something both Diane and Lorraine had personally witnessed. Even though Diane expressed how demoralising and frustrating it was for her to commonly hear Romany-Gypsies addressed as, "the dirty gyppos" and "the pikey's", she felt that ignoring the use of such derogatory ethnic slurs was the better option for the security of her job. And I can't say I disagree, and nor can I blame her for keeping her ethnic heritage hidden in the closet.

My Gran, who had been a hard-working, up-standing member of society, a kind person who would literally share her last slice of bread with anyone in need, could have easily been denied care at home. Due to the care staff, in Sevenoaks Kent, who had point-blank refused to visit the site where she lived. If it wasn't for Diane, accompanying the other carers, and giving reassurance, that my Granny was no different than any other terminally ill elderly lady, we would have faced a fight to ensure my Granny was provided the care she needed to die peacefully in her own home. It is known, by our experiences personally had, that professional people from within all sectors commonly hold a bias about delivering their services when it's a Romany-Gypsy in need. Such racist discrimination cannot be denied.

Above photo: My Granny-Dinkey, (on the left) and me in 2012. "Always in my heart and mind."

I cherished every moment I have ever spent with everyone from the older generations especially my Granny-Dinkey. I preferred keeping their company than being in the company of my own age group. I would say for Louisa and me that our teenage years were enriched by spending so much time with our grandparents. Also, living on the site with my husband's grandparents has enriched my life by having the opportunity to spend so much time with them that I thought of them and loved them no differently than my other Grandparents. Louisa's granny (Aunt Sissy) also lived on my site. We were blessed to have the time we did with our older generations they taught us that the kindness to be generous is a blessing.

Louisa had asked me to help her organise a concert to raise money for the families (refugees) she had seen, walking alongside the road in 2015. She had already chosen the songs and we asked the children from the church Louisa attended and the children living on my site, to sing at the concert. She had phoned me to make sure I was going to church the following Sunday because she would be announcing that the tickets were on sale. Louisa was nervous about speaking publicly for the first time, and she wanted me there for moral support.

Louisa overcame her fears, and not only did she speak in the church, but she also went on to introduce the singers at the concert and spoke about the refugees and their plight. Louisa had said to me many times during the run-up to the concert, that £500 was the amount she wanted to raise, and she knew God was going to let her get it, and do you know what I witnessed? To the exact pound that was the amount raised! The concert was a complete success and all who attended enjoyed themselves.

For both Louisa and I, this is how our spiritual relationship works. An injustice is felt empathetically, we brainstorm ideas of how to help and then we put our time and energy into making those ideas become a reality. We both know and have learned, that through love, compassion, empathy, and determination anything is possible.

Louisa and I have disagreed about the Bible's writings and about who and what God is, for decades. Yet we have never had a single falling out, never had a cross word either, regardless of our different views and that's because love doesn't allow judgment. Love instead accepts in understanding.

My memories of being a young girl staying at my Grandparent's for the weekend, was made more exciting for me when Ricky, Grandfarver's Gorger Christian friend, would visit. It would not take long for Grandfarver and Ricky to debate the Bible's writings. I grew up in an era where children did not interrupt an adult conversation, but this did have its advantages it taught me to listen - and listen I did.

Ricky would read the Bible to my Grandfarver, (who could not read or write and to sign his name he would mark the page with a cross). Ricky would always request to read the Bible from the New Testament, but Grandfarver preferred to have the story read from its beginning. Sitting comfortably on the floor Grandfarver would have one leg raised, serving as a table rest for his arm which would be holding his cup of sweet black tea and in his other hand would be a tobacco roll-up. Grandfarver would want to understand if there were any reasons given to why the stories about the Abrahamic God portrayed him as a wicked God. Poor Ricky, who was a devout Christian, had his work cut out to defend and justify what he was reading.

I learned from listening to Ricky that the Devil has many names: Satan, Lucifer, Beelzebub, the dragon, the light bearer and even more. He is the most beautiful of all God's creations, and possibly a guardian cherub; it was confusing visualising the Devil as a cherub because my mind's eye conjured up the image of beautiful chubby babies who played harps or hit humans with cupid's arrows. God had created his archangel perfect, wise, talented, skilled, and beautiful.

Yet, at some point, and I don't know when or how this happened, Lucifer was found to have iniquity in his heart and desired to become God because he wanted to rule, he didn't want to be under God's authority. God told Lucifer that he couldn't become a ruler and Lucifer started a rebellion against God and some of the other angels allied with Lucifer instead of staying loyal to their creator.

THE MYSTERY IN BEING A GYPSY

Lucifer's iniquity in his heart, according to the Bible's writings, resulted in a third of God's angels falling from heaven. Grandfarver questioned why God, who is all-seeing and all-knowing, had created Satan in the first place. Obviously, Ricky couldn't give the answer to a question that only God himself would know the answer to. Ricky read the story of Adam and Eve and I can recall word for word my Grandfarver's questioning,

"So God created Adam and Eve. He must have loved them like I love my children and my little grandbabies?"

Ricky agreed that indeed God would love his creations as much, and if not even more.

Grandfarver would continue, "So, God created a beautiful garden, a perfect paradise and he allowed them to eat from every tree but forbid them to eat from the tree of knowledge, is this correct?"

"Yes, that's right Nelson," Ricky would answer.

But my Grandfarver could not understand why God would not want his children to be knowledgeable. Especially when Satan, his adversary, had access to ways to target Adam and Eve. Nor could he understand why God forbade Adam and Eve from eating from the tree of knowledge in the first place – which, as he saw it, would give them the ability to discern good from evil for themselves.

Grandfarver could only look at God from his own perspective, a father's one: as the protector. He could not comprehend when being 'all-seeing' and 'all-knowing', that any father would choose to allow the serpent (the Devil) to deceive Eve into eating from his forbidden tree.

He questioned, "If God didn't want his human children, to eat from the tree of knowledge then why didn't he stop Satan, does it say why in the Bible? Did God warn his children about his best creation Lucifer?"

Ricky did his best to explain it as he had been taught it. He believed God allowed this to happen because he had allowed Adam and Eve to have their own 'free will' and he informed my Grandfarver that it doesn't say in the bible that God warned or taught Adam and Eve about his adversary. Grandfarver contested Ricky's reasoning because according to the Bible it was God who had forbidden them to eat from the tree of knowledge and without discernment of good and evil it was easy for Lucifer to entice Eve.

My Grandfarver valued the importance of teaching children knowledge because in doing so they will be better equipped to make good, informed choices for themselves. Also, as a dad and a grandfather, it was difficult for him to accept that God, as the father to us all, would allow Lucifer access and power over Adam and Eve (and all humans), to be able to deceive them because Satan has power over all nations of the earth.

Grandfarver's challenges made against the Bible's writings was because, as he saw it, first God did nothing to stop his adversary and after allowing this to happen, he then chose to punish his children for not obeying him. The punishment for Adam and Eves disobedience is death. But this was not an isolated punishment for Adam and Eve alone, God's punishment of death was cast onto all humans.

Even though I grew up listening to my Grandfarver-Nelson's plausible questioning, it didn't stop me from becoming a Christian.

I used to go to church regularly. I loved the communal singing and anything that was connected to raising money to help those who are less fortunate. But as soon as I had my son at 22 years of age my world was centred around him. He was everything, and all that mattered. He kept my life very busy and perfectly fulfilled. My life took on a different direction, as a mother, away from religiously attending church and religiously reading the Bible.

My Dad and Grandfarver have been two of the most influential men in my life. They have taught me to question, to listen and more importantly 'without evidence' to think for myself.

My Dad also taught me one of my greatest life lessons, "Judging others is easy to do and will keep us busy gossiping but to understand others - now that's a harder challenge to accomplish."

8

FORCED TO USE THE SWORD

When my son was around 7 years old. I received a letter from his school. It contained information about a production theatre company who were going to perform for the children and staff at River Primary. The information in the letter contained the names of the performances, 'Tommy, the Gypsy boxer' and 'The Fourth Nail' with the date and times of when they'd be performed. As soon as I had finished reading the letter, for a reason I hadn't yet rationalised, I had a negative feeling in my stomach. If I had to describe the feeling, I would choose to do so using the analogy of sound; it's like a bell ringing a warning. It can be a hugely uncomfortable negative feeling, or a small feeling of negativity warning that something is slightly off. Life has taught me to listen when the warning bells ring!

My over-active, questioning thought process had been triggered. Why did this play have to include my ethnicity? In my life experience when Gorgers (non-Romany) make TV programmes or write stories about us, they have largely left us having to deal with the backlash from their portrayal of my ethnic group. Would a play be any different?

I thought I should call and ask Kate if she knew anything about this play. I had not met Kate but because she worked for the Traveller Education Services, I had heard about her from others who had praised her name as being kind, helpful and non-discriminatory. I got hold of Kate's number and rang to explain about the letter asking if she knew what the play 'Tommy, the Gypsy Boxer' would entail. I went on to share my thoughts and questions. Kate listened with kindness, and she was certainly committed to giving me her time. Our call ended with her promise that she would find out what the play was about and get back to me.

A few days later Kate called me back informing me that the play about Tommy was a story of a Gypsy lad, who makes a success of his life through fighting and the second performance, 'The Fourth Nail' included characters who are also being presented as people from my ethnic group.

Kate told me, "The Forth Nail is a story about a Gypsy blacksmith who made the nails to crucify Jesus." She continued to further explain, "I believe these performances will help promote theatre as entertainment, to the next generation."

Kate disagreed with me that there was anything to be concerned with and I could only agree: it was all about the promotion for theatre companies.

The bigger picture for me was feeling very strongly that these performances could help contribute to more negative stereotypes and discrimination for my ethnic group, but Kate couldn't share my concerns, at this time.

With further research, I discovered that 'The Fourth Nail' was a play about a Gypsy blacksmith who forged the nails to crucify Christ. As the myth, legend is told the Gypsy blacksmith made the first three nails, two of which were for each one of Christ's hands, and the third nail would be used to drive his feet together. The Fourth Nail was going to be used to drive through the heart of Jesus; serving as the final and fatal blow that would ensure his death.

The blacksmith made the first three nails without any complications but upon placing the fourth nail into the water to cool it down - it remained hot. He tried again and again to cool the nail to no avail. This myth tells the story that Gypsies were then cursed to travel, never again being allowed to settle permanently. And no matter where the blacksmith went, the hot nail followed him, tauntingly burning him and forcing him to shift (move on). The conscious ability of the nail was from the power of 'God's curse' which forcibly made the blacksmith and all Gypsies eternal wanderers thereafter.

I discovered that there are different variations to the story of 'The Fourth Nail'. One reads that God sent an angel to tell the Gypsy blacksmith that the Roman soldiers were going to order him

THE MYSTERY IN BEING A GYPSY

to forge the nails and that he would be paid to make four. The angel of God instructed the Gypsy blacksmith, "You have been commanded by God to only hand over three of the nails, to prevent the fatal blow into Jesus's heart." As a reward for doing this God gave Gypsies the right of passage to roam freely.

Another variation reads that a different Gypsy man had stolen the fourth nail, to mend his wagon. Because this theft had resulted in saving Jesus from having the nail driven into his heart, God would make allowances and would turn a blind eye to the sin of theft. Allowing Gypsies, forever more, to steal without being held accountable.

I have been accustomed to hearing many myths and legends regarding Romanies, but this was the first time I had heard about the tale of 'The Fourth Nail'. Discovering this information, I understood the intuitive warning bell I felt when I first opened the letter.

I also learned there are sadly Romany in different countries, who actually believe this tale to be true; believing all who share our ethnic origin have been cursed by God.

I was mulling over what steps I should take next, because I had a deep routed negative feeling that nothing good would come from having these plays performed. What would children, of primary school age, (where the majority still believe in Father Christmas and the tooth fairy), start believing about Romany-Gypsies? I could not comprehend how children from this age group would have the ability to use their 'own' due diligence to decipher the stories, in the plays presented, as fiction and understand the plays were simply a theatre entertainment promotion.

In the evening my cousin Nelson had called for a chat, and I told him about the plays. He shared my concerns immediately, without me having to explain them to him. He was also in disbelief that primary schools had allowed such performances to be shown and suggested I write a letter to my sons Headmistress making my concerns known.

This would be the second 'formal' letter that I had found myself needing to write, and because this would be read by professional teachers, I felt apprehensive about having to do so. I wanted to be taken seriously and felt that spelling, punctuation, and grammar needed to be perfect for the professionals to consider my concerns as valid.

It was Friday evening, and I knew I had to act quickly because we didn't have long till the date of the performances. I didn't have the time to wait for Kevin's weekly Wednesday visit, so he could proofread for me. I explained this to Nelson, and he then asked his wife to help me, and she assisted me to write………

Dear Mrs. Potter,

I am writing to you to express my concerns about the upcoming performances scheduled to be shown at Riverview. I understand the theatre company will perform two performances. One entitled, 'Tommy the Gypsy Boxer' which tells the story of a boy who makes a success of his life by boxing. Culturally, our children are raised to protect themselves and most boys and even our girls are taught to defend themselves. This story certainly does nothing to encourage and aspire Romany-Gypsy pupils to become academics. I feel performances shown within the school setting should at least have some educational value and not simply be about promotion for theatre companies.

The second performance entitled, 'The Fourth Nail' is an allegorical story, that before receiving the letter from Riverview, I had never heard of. When researching I have learned that this is a myth which portrays Gypsies as being the enemy of Christendom. This tale explains how a Gypsy blacksmith took part in aiding the Romans to commit the crime of murdering Christ. As punishment for the Gypsy blacksmith's involvement, all Gypsies are forevermore doomed, by God's curse to be nomads.

My concerns are first foremost as a mother with a son in your care. Secondly, I am concerned also for the other children in Riverview. We are a church of England school and I hold misgivings that once this play is performed it could be adopted, in the learning minds of children, as fact!

Who would be held responsible, if there were repercussions towards the Romany-Gypsy pupils at Riverview, should they experience any type of bullying, physical, mental, or emotional abuse as a direct result of these plays? I am writing to ask that you reconsider allowing these plays to be shown due to the concerns raised.
Yours sincerely.

Kate called to tell me that writing the letter had caused a stir because Riverview had already committed to having the plays shown. It had been considered appropriate because other primary schools had already allowed the theatre company to perform. I asked if I could watch the rehearsals.

Kate replied, "I would also be interested to see these plays for myself, I will find out if this is possible."

When Kate got back in touch, she did so to inform me she would be permitted to watch the plays but unfortunately, an invite had not been extended to me. It was felt by Traveller Education Services that I should, 'Trust the Professionals'.

Kate and her colleagues watched the rehearsals and gave their feedback. After this, I received a call from Mrs. Potter (the headmistress) who informed me that after having a conversation with a senior member from Traveller Education Services she had decided to not allow 'The Fourth Nail' to be performed for her children at Riverview. However, she would personally view the Riverview rehearsal of 'Tommy the Gypsy Boxer', and she extended an invite to me to receive my feedback.

My husband and I arrived at the school, where we were greeted by Mrs. Potter. We then walked through the school into the children's playground where the theatre touring bus was already in position and set up for their rehearsal to perform later that day. We took a seat and waited for the show to start. The female performers wore brightly coloured costumes and headbands of gold coins, an old fashion style of the Romany, which has become a stereotype. I let out a sigh and Mrs. Potter responded explaining apologetically that she had taken it for granted that the plays would be fun and that they would simply help promote theatre entertainment to the next generation. And because this theatre company had performed in so many other primaries this had served as reassurance that the shows would be suitable for our children at Riverview.

Mrs. Potter told me she had learned a valuable lesson, and she was hoping the Tommy play would be appropriate.

I respected her honesty when she said, "I have found myself in a difficult position because of the short space of time from receiving your letter to the scheduled performance day. My staff had already been given the allocated performance time off work, and many had made alternative commitments."

I sympathised and agreed that we were short on time for a perfect resolve. We were both hoping for the Tommy play to pass as 'okay'.

Once the show had finished Mrs. Potter asked, "What do you think?"

I simply replied, "Good luck in break time because you're going to have plenty of boisterous children now play fighting."

Kate's become a friend, she was everything and much more, of the praise given by all who know her. Mrs. Potter and I also formed a close relationship, one where I became a trusted staff member in her school as a Teaching Assistant (TA). The theatre performers told Mrs. Potter, "I'd been the 'only' brick wall they had encountered".

This made me feel disappointed because I wished they'd have faced at least some hurdles along the way, before encountering me, "The Brick Wall". The truth for me, in all this was - I had a bad feeling from the start. My concern was how my ethnicity was going to be portrayed into the young and impressionable minds of the next generation.

My original concern from reading the letter could be viewed as having a bad feeling because of the mistrust I have of all decision makers in authority. It could also be viewed as a spiritual gut feeling of intuition. I would say it was both. But either way, from the moment I read the letter I felt something was wrong.

When I came to learn that 'The Fourth Nail', also included my ethnicity and it was about a Gypsy blacksmith who forged the nails that were used to crucify Jesus I became anxious feeling that this play would be responsible, in laying the foundation for the future 'unconscious intolerance' to be planted in the 'innocent' minds of children to be bias against my ethnic group. It most certainly would have helped to reinforce a dangerous ideology, many Gorger people already own, believing 'all' Romany-Gypsies should be held accountable (on suspicion, fact, or fiction) for any wrong any Gypsy commits - or is accused of - by default of ethnicity.

I enjoyed the years I spent working at Riverview and I learned many good parenting skills. And because most of the Romany-Gypsy children, at Riverview, were not originally allowed to go on school trips (due to the trust issues their parents hold towards professionals), my time working there saw the children being allowed on the school trips when they were placed in my care.

I have found myself needing to explain, many times over, to too many professional people, that our trust issues are deep-rooted from intergenerational trauma. And when knowing our history, our mistrust is justified and then understood.

My son received a good education at Riverview and so did my daughter. When she was nine years old, I had returned home from a painfully tedious meeting of 'Gypsy and Traveller statistics', just in time to collect her from school.

My daughter bounced out of school telling me, "I have had a really good day." Experiencing a fried brain from the meeting I hadn't questioned why and instead replied, "That's lovely I'm pleased you had a nice day my princess."

The following week she again came bouncing out of school saying what a good day she had. This time I questioned with interest to find out what she had been doing that pleased her so much. My daughter explained that she had been in a classroom with other children making crafts. Questioning her some more, I found out the other children in this crafts class were also Romany-Gypsies.

Once we were home, I called the school and spoke with the receptionist to make further enquires. I was then informed the school was taking part in the Gypsy, Roma, and Traveller (GRT) History Month. I had never heard of this before, so I used the internet and found out that 'GRT History Month' takes place in June and had begun three years prior in 2008. The purpose is intended to help tackle prejudice, challenge myths, and amplify the voices of Gypsies, Roma, and Travellers within wider society.

The next morning, at the school drop off, I requested to have a quick word with my daughter's teacher, I wanted to know what lessons had been missed whilst my daughter had attended the 'GRT History Month' session. Receiving the reply, I instantly decided I didn't want my child to participate once a week, for four consecutive weeks, in what was in all honesty a crafts session for the Romany-Gypsy pupils of Riverview. I told her teacher, "I don't want my daughter removed from her maths lessons."

Her teacher showed her disappointment in her facial expression, and I did understand Riverview had tried to celebrate 'GRT History Month' with good intent. However, the 'GRT History Month', in primaries, involved taking the known Gypsy, Roma and Traveller children from their curriculum lessons, allowing them to be creative about their ethnicity and culture. It's a nice token gesture but segregating children by ethnicity into their own session, will help achieve nothing to challenge myths or tackle prejudice. I also advised Riverview staff, to seek permission from all parents whose children have been attending the GRT History session.

I know parents who are happy for their children to participate in the 'GRT History Month' activities, but there's also many more who have not chosen for their children to participate. However, for me, I feel the decisions made to introduce 'GRT History Month' was agreed with little more commitment than to appease the ethnic participants who were involved with the decision making. Three groups have been placed together, two of which are totally separate ethnic groups whose origin, language and history are not the same, and the third group are first- and second-generation Eastern European Roma.

'GRT History Month' was started in the London Borough of Brent in 2001, and was endorsed by Parliament in 2007, and has been celebrated nationally since 2008. Since then, the Greater London Authority has partnered with other Gypsy, Roma, Traveller organisations to hold an annual GRT History Month event in June.

I feel it would be a difficult task to educate primary-aged school children to help tackle prejudice, challenge myths, and amplify the voices of Gypsies, Roma, and Travellers within wider society. I believe such changes need to be made from the top down not the bottom up beginning with 5-year-olds. Also, I would not appreciate my child learning all the horrors of the Holocaust or about the centuries of persecution, slavery, and racism that Romanies have endured. My personal preference is that young minds should stay living in the land of magic and fairy tales for as long as possible.

As my Granny-Dinky would say, "We're a long-time adults."

In all honestly, because Romany-Gypsies lives have been shaped, influenced, and forced down roads – many would have never chosen to travel – but were instead forced to travel due to racism and persecution, it's impossible to give a fair and balanced account without telling the horrific details of our history. The segregation of Gypsy children within education for any reason, I am completely against – even if this is widely accepted and believed to be an attempt at inclusion.

9

A PROTEST, CONFERENCES & A CALLING

My friend Louisa and I went to our first protest in London, in 2015, against the planning definition change. The Government had proposed to update the Planning Policy for Gypsy sites. This proposal would change the definition of 'Gypsy', to no longer include those who have ceased travelling permanently for any reason including work commitments, education, old age, disabilities, or ill health. This was a Policy which was disingenuously disguised as not being racist. We are a legitimate ethnic group who cannot be defined by where or how we live. Yet, this Planning Policy redefined our ethnicity to being nothing more than a people group who live a nomadic lifestyle.

Nelson Jack Boswell said, in his open letter to the Government, "This law has been thought up by many tyrants, evil and ungodly people. If we take a French man and put him in a cave, on a ship, or in a trailer (caravan) he is still a French man because that is his race, his culture, his breed." (Full letter can be read in the Travellers' Times, 'I am Tatchna Rumney Chell', 24th of June 2016. www.travellerstimes.org.uk).

We met Joseph Jones at this protest (a Romany-Gypsy gentleman) who had a lot to offer us, by way of advice and teaching us about the system. Joseph, who I address as 'Uncle Joe' as a show of respect, (which is a cultural practice that's spanned the ages whereby people who are from our parents' generation are titled Aunt or Uncle). Uncle Joe opened my eyes to a world where despite every effort, we have been taking one step forward and two steps back. Louisa and I had faith in protests and petitions back then, but they made no difference and achieved nothing!

However, we did learn that the Traveller Movement (TM), who had organised the protest, are a charity for Romany-Gypsies, Roma, and Irish Travellers, neither Louisa nor I nor anyone we knew had heard of TM before.

I was pleasantly surprised to learn The Traveller Movement (TM) have been established since 1999, with supporting Travellers and challenging discrimination. Uncle Joe recommended I read the Travellers' Times article which reported on TM winning a discrimination case against Romany-Gypsies and Irish Travellers.

Travellers' Times is a multi-award-winning media focusing on things that matter to Gypsy, Roma, and Traveller people. In their own words and I quote: Travellers' Times are dedicated to stand in a direct challenge to one-sided views of Gypsy, Roma, and Travellers.

The following is a copy of the article printed in the Travellers' Times that explains what took place:

The Traveller Movement charity has won a landmark victory in the High Court and dealt a crushing blow to casual racism against Gypsies and Travellers after Justice Hand ruled that a JD Wetherspoons pub in North London, acted illegally when it refused entry to Travellers on the grounds of their race. The incident happened in November 2011 at the Coronet, on Holloway Road, when a group of delegates from the Traveller Movement's annual conference attempted to enter the pub but were stopped by door staff.

JD Wetherspoon, which is Britain's largest pub chain with over 900 pubs across the UK, will have to pay costs and damages to the group after the presiding judge ruled that its staff had stopped them from entering the pub on racial grounds. The delegates included Travellers, a Police Inspector, a Barrister, and a priest, all of whom were claimants in the case. The group was only allowed to enter the pub to speak to the manager when Inspector Watson produced his Police identity card - and only on the condition that he was responsible for the group.

Martin Howe, senior partner of Howe and Co Solicitors, was in the group who were turned away by door staff and was also a claimant in the case. "This judgment will shake to the core all those who engage in racist conduct towards Irish Travellers and

Romany-Gypsies. The last bastion of 'acceptable racism' has come crashing down," he said.

"We are overjoyed with today's decision," said Yvonne MacNamara, CEO of the Traveller Movement. "Justice has finally been done for those who were turned away from the Coronet pub because they were Travellers, or because they were associated with Travellers. In this day and age, it is outrageous that a national pub chain like JD Wetherspoons can carry out such a blatant act of discrimination against members of the Romany-Gypsy and Traveller communities, their friends and colleagues. As a national charity who works to promote equality for Gypsies and Travellers across the country, we too often come across members of these communities being refused access to goods and services on the grounds of their ethnicity. We hope Justice Hand's decision will mark a sea of change in the unacceptably high levels of discrimination these communities experience." (Full article can be read at: JD Wetherspoon guilty of racism against Travellers. 18th of May 2018 www.travellerstimes.org.uk).

After the protest, I was busy attending back-to-back meetings to learn all I could. The doors to a world I did not even know existed, had opened. I attended the Surrey, Gypsy, Traveller, Communities, Forum (SGTCF) where I was asked to join them as a committee member, and shortly after I was offered the position of 'Lead in Education' which I happily accepted. The Co-Chair Hilda Brazil or the Treasurer John Hockley would regularly hold the SGTCF committee meetings in their homes. During one of these meetings, when speaking to John, he brought to my attention that there were not many 'known' Gypsy or Traveller registered foster carers.

It is customary, within our culture, when there are children who cannot be taken care of by their parents, the responsibility automatically falls to their grandparents or another family member. It got me thinking about children in care, if there was a lack of known foster carers, then these children wouldn't have the opportunity to be placed within their own ethnic kin.

I had attended a local NHS stop smoking advisors' meeting as part of my work position for the SGTCF. Where a lady approached me and asked if I had access to the 'GRT community'. I assumed, without asking, that she must have overheard me speaking about working for the SGTCF.

The acronym 'GRT' for Gypsy, Roma, and Traveller, I discovered, is regularly used in the professional and political world. However, in the experiences of Romany-Gypsies, this acronym has helped to promote an already existing 'false' belief that Romany-Gypsies are simply a nomadic community. And considering we have a 500-year plus documented history, and DNA evidence proving even longer such false beliefs can only point to an outdated ignorance because we 'are' a legitimate ethnic group.

Our ethnicity cannot be changed regardless of where or how we live, be that: on a council or privately owned site; living on land which is owned or rented; living in a house which is owned or rented; in a trailer, mobile, challey, or if you are Alfie Best (the Romany-Gypsy self-made billionaire) in a mansion!

The home lived in is totally irrelevant to our ethnic heritage. It's already gotten to a point where the 'GRT Community' or the 'Travelling Community' is viewed as being the Politically Correct (PC) term to racially identify us, and this PC terminology has 'incorrectly' been adopted across all professional sectors, and within politics. But 'GRT' isn't legally representative of our ethnicity. In fact, the term 'Gypsy' as well as the term 'Traveller' can and are increasingly used to represent the 'the travelling communities' in general (anyone who lives a partial or full nomadic lifestyle regardless of ethnicity).

Romany-Gypsy is our legal ethnic term (in the UK) and I feel the need to stress again, "We Are a Legitimate Ethnic Group."

I didn't explain this to the lady at the NHS meeting, because I knew there was no disrespect intended. It's just what she, along with many others, have been led to believe or taught to be correct.

I simply replied that I did have access. She then explained that she had been carrying around bumper stickers that advertised for GRT people to consider fostering, in the hope of meeting someone who would be able to hand them out because she didn't have access to the GRT community. She requested if would I be kind enough to give the stickers out. I told her I could place them on the tables that are laid out in meetings, where there's always a stash of leaflets. I can only assume these bumper stickers had materialised because of another 'Gypsy project' where funding was bid for and received, by Gorgers, and where this idea was thought to be a brilliant one, without having any input from ethnic members. Whatever decisions were made, or whoever was involved in producing the bumper stickers, clearly didn't have an agenda considering they ended up being left in a handbag before being given to me!

Later when I left the meeting, on my journey home, I found myself 'again' thinking about Romany-Gypsy children in care. For children who'd been raised in a tight-knit community of growing up on a site with extended family and relatives, what a culture shock it must be for them to be placed in a house. I wondered if such children would feel the same way as people in prison do caged and initialised. Only these children were innocent, they would have committed no crimes.

Mark Haythorne, who was the Project Officer of 'GRT Brighter Futures' and also a committee member of SGTCF, invited me to accompany him to Ash Manor School, in Surrey. That's when I first met Billiejo Sines, a Romany-Gypsy woman who worked in the school as a key worker. Mark and I also met the Deputy Head Jo Luhman who was now teaching second-generation Romany-Gypsy and other Traveller children. Jo was keen to point out that the sole reason her Gypsy and Traveller pupils do well at Ash Manor is because they are an inclusive school.

Jo Luhman stated, "We are a community, and we respect all. Everybody has an equal opportunity to decide what they want in their life, and we will support them to achieve that."

When I arrived back home, after visiting the school, I contacted my friend Lisa Smith, who works at Travellers' Times. I told her there's a school who are doing so well for our children that it's worthy of praise. Lisa spoke to her colleagues, then Steven Horne, a writer for Travellers' Times, went along to interview Jo (Deputy Head) and Billiejo Sines (Key Worker). It was a pleasure to witness a school worthy of praise getting some recognition. The article 'Equal and Empowered' was published in the Travellers' Times on the 18th of October 2016, www.travellerstimes.org.uk.

Once I became more acquainted with Jo Luhman, she asked if I'd like to become a governor at Ash Manor School. Being true to myself, I asked to have some time to think about it, but I did agree to attend their next governor's meeting, as a trial run, to help me decide. By this time Ash Manor had a new Head Teacher rather than the one, Jo Luhman had worked under for many years as the Deputy Head. At the governors meeting, it was said that many parents were feeling resentment about the 'special treatment' the Traveller children were receiving at the school. I highlighted the importance for the school, regardless of the complaints received, to remain inclusive of their Romany-Gypsy and other Traveller pupils, particularly in relation to the cultural celebrations and teachings that their Deputy Head (Jo Luhman) had included.

I stated, "Where there's nothing for children to identify with, then they have been excluded, and inclusion should never be viewed as a special treatment!"

I shared with the Governors, "When I was taught about the Holocaust within the education system, there was no mention about the nazis determination to ethnically cleanse Romany people, and few people know Romany-Gypsies have a recorded history, in our country spanning over 500 years."

I also expressed what I believed Ash Manor did well. I praised the commitment and dedication of their Deputy Head Jo Luhman. Her passion and effort had resulted in trust being built between the school staff and parents. The hiring of Billie-Jo, as an ethnic community member, was a wise choice that was just as beneficial for the pupils as it was for the teaching staff and the parents.

When the parents were welcomed into Ash Manor and their children's ethnicity was recognised and celebrated for the centuries of survival against all the odds. Where our history was taught and the door for communication was open, the parents themselves engaged and support their children's education.

Because first, there must be trust before there is any understanding of value.

I only attended that one single governor's meeting. I had committed so much of my time advocating to make a change, for the inclusive education of Romany-Gypsies that I couldn't face the possibility of this school's inclusiveness being eradicated. This school had managed an inclusive education for all. The years of hard work by Jo Luman and her colleagues had paid off and the results spoke for themselves. But with Jo accepting her new job, as Head Teacher in a different school, without needing a crystal ball, I feared I could see into the future. If any changes were made to appease those who felt the inclusiveness of our history and culture was special treatment, then the Gypsy and Traveller pupils would probably no longer strive and learn at the pace they'd been academically achieving. I just couldn't witness up close and personal; what I believed the future could hold for Ash Manor's Romany-Gypsy and other Traveller children. To potentially see them no longer obtain an 'inclusive education' was more than I could bear to stay around and witness. So, I declined the offer to become a Governor at Ash Manor School.

At one of our SGTCF committee meetings Hilda Brazil, and Anne Wilson shared with me a story about a young single mother, who'd gotten herself in trouble for stealing. We agreed there was the hope of finding a placement for her children to be able to stay together, while the mother was in prison. We were committed to helping if we could.

My heart ached to find out this single mother, who had no family support in England (because all her family lived in Ireland), had been caught stealing food, babies' milk, and nappies. I found it truly heart-breaking that she had stolen for need, because she had certainly not stolen for the greed of financial gain. Having had previous convictions for stealing similar items the judge had reluctantly given her a custodial sentence. The mother's only concern was that while her children were being looked after by the state, that they could be kept together during her six-week prison sentence. Social Services had contacted some of the Gypsy and Traveller charities and organisations to find out if there were any Irish Traveller foster carers, who could take these children in.

I was so emotionally affected hearing about this family, it made no difference to me that these children were not from my own ethnic group. I just wanted to care for them myself. Again, the notion of fostering was at the forefront of my mind I began seriously considering it. The only hurdle I could think of was bonding with the children and the pain of then parting with them when the time came. What effect would that have on me?

Was I emotionally strong enough to cope with giving the children back?

I spoke with my husband and told him I believed, in a case like this, of short-term fostering, that I felt more than capable of caring for the children and would not be affected when it was time to hand them back to their parent. He agreed this was something he could see me doing and said he would support my decision, believing it was my decision to make because I would be the stay-at-home parent.

A desire was growing my heart to become a foster carer, and I had begun looking into and seriously considering this possibility. It had come up on three separate occasions, at three different meetings where fostering and adoption had no relation to the agenda. I was beginning to believe these were signs of a calling. The number three means something to me

THE MYSTERY IN BEING A GYPSY

spiritually, it means to take notice of the signs, because these signs have always led me to do the worthiest work of all: compassionate work of love.

I found out from my friend Hayley (Roberts), who has been fostering for a number of years, what it takes to become a qualified registered foster parent.

10

OUR DESTINY CHILD

I received a call from my Mum informing me that she had just found out that her sister's granddaughter (Essie) was in care of the state. Essie and her parents had lived opposite my Mum, and Granny-Dinkey for a while and during this time my Mum and Essie had formed a close relationship. Mum explained that her nephew (Essie's dad) had been visited by Social Services who had served the relevant papers to him, so they could apply to the courts for a long-term fostering order for Essie. At which point, Essie's dad panic shared this information with his immediate family - who in turn told my Mum.

Mum further explained her sister (Essie's grandmother) had contacted Social Services asking if any members from her side of the family could be considered for Kinship Care. When our call ended, I instantly had a flashback to the only memory I have of Essie. She would have been about three years old and was playing, in my Granny-Dinkey's Garden. I had tried to engage with her, but she was far too interested in playing on the swings and slides. After seeing this flashback memory, in my mind's eye, I felt an overwhelming sense of sadness. I then began thinking about how little Essie would be coping. Being removed from everything that had been her life, it must be daunting, to say the least.

I spoke with my Mum again later in the day, by this time all of my Mum's lot (family) now knew about Essie's situation. My Mum, my Aunt Julie's family and my sister Sarah's family had decided to put their names forward to be assessed.

I spoke to my husband about Essie's situation when he came home from work, and he was also upset to hear the news. I explained Mum, my Sarah, and Aunt Julie had all put their names forward to be assessed for her Kinship Care. Dan's reply was quite matter of fact and he said that we should do the same. The idea of being assessed to get Essie had already crossed my mind, since I heard about her situation earlier in the day. However, I'm not an impulsive person and I had already rationalized, if we were going to consider putting our names forward, then we should talk about it as a family, with both of our children discussing what this could mean for us all. Dan and I agreed to speak about it again once we heard back from my Mum, to see if any of my relatives would be considered.

Our conversation continued about Essie because we couldn't understand why our side of the family was only just now hearing about her situation considering she had been in state care for several weeks. From the little we had just learned Essie had not been in her mum's sister's care prior to being placed in state care.

Over the next two weeks, more information about Essie was being shared. Margaret Queen (Essie's social worker) said upfront that my Mum wouldn't be considered because of her age. My Aunt Julie had been speaking directly with Essie's social worker Margaret, and through my Aunt Julie we discovered that Essie had been living with one of her mother's relatives, who had cared for her for a few months, prior to her being given into state care.

When Essie's parents moved from the site (where my Granny and Mum lived) into a house they separated a while after. Essie's dad then moved back onto the site, while Essie remained living with her mum in their house. It was no secret that Essie's mum struggled with drug addiction, and we understood Essie was being cared for, largely, by her aunt (her mum's sister). And that was all we knew. Essie was little more than a stranger to Dan and me.

Essie was on my mind and in my heart. I kept visualising, the only time I had seen her, when she was playing with the other children in Gran's Garden. I rang my Aunt Julie and shared with her that Dan and I had been considering putting our names forward to be assessed. We had spoken with both of our children, who were happy to have Essie come live with us. I asked my Aunt Julie if I could have the social worker's number, but she told me that Margaret had explained she would only have time to do two assessments. It looked as though it had been assumed by Social Services that none of the dad's side of the family was interested in taking on Kinship Care of Essie.

My Sarah rang me the next day and told me she had been given an appointment date to be assessed, this made us both feel hopeful. Aunt Julie had also received her appointment which was on the same day as my Sarah's assessment. Margaret was ringing my sister back to conduct a pre-telephone assessment. Things were happening fast.

After my Sarah passed her telephone assessment she asked Margaret, "Is it worth doing the home visit assessment because the date for the Judge to rule has already been set?"

Margaret assured my sister that, if she passed the home assessment, she would certainly be considered because they prefer family placement.

I rang Aunt Julie knowing her pre-telephone assessment would have also been conducted, and just from the sound of her voice I could tell she was disappointed.

Margaret had informed her it wasn't worth doing her home assessment because the recommendations were that Essie was to have a bedroom of her own, even though, within family placements, this isn't commonly necessary. But in Essie's case, because Julie lived in the same Borough as her parents, and worked outside of school hours, these three factors would contribute to a failed assessment. Aunt Julie had then spontaneously taken the opportunity to explain about Dan and me. She told Margaret that her niece and husband would like to be considered and that she believed we would be more suitable to meet the Social Services requirements. Her response was a firm, "No".

Margaret then asked my Aunt Julie, "How many more of the dad's side of the family are going to crawl out of the woodwork?"

Of course, this was a rhetorical question and one that did not give us any hope that Dan and I would even be considered. My Aunt Julie was persistent in stressing to Margaret that we would be brilliant, telling her I have worked with children, been a teacher and lived

THE MYSTERY IN BEING A GYPSY

outside the county, and could also accommodate Essie with her own bedroom. Margaret's answer was still no. To be honest, I was disgruntled to hear the social worker's response and her remark about "crawling out of the woodwork".

I felt a pang of guilt as I put the phone down and I thought, "I should have put our names forward the day we found out - when Dan said we should."

I had to try, I'd send a pleading email, I'd beg if I had to. I sent up a prayer, "God, if we are what this innocent child needs, and she is supposed to be here with us, then make it possible. I will do all I can, but I only want this child if we are what she needs, Amen". I Googled Kent Council's email address and no sooner had I done so, I was already writing...

Dear Margaret,

I'd like to introduce myself. My name is Genty Lee. I am the person Julie (my aunt) was referring to, as hopefully, being eligible for an assessment for the possible Kinship Care of Essie.

I feel it's important to let you know that my family and I are willing and able to open our home to become Essie's. I want to make it very clear that much thought and consideration has been taken before deciding to contact you. The possibility of Essie becoming a family member is something we, as a family, have agreed on. Should you choose to allow us the opportunity, we would be more than happy to go ahead with an assessment.

I understand Essie has been pushed from pillar to post and that there will be concerns about placing her with yet another relative. However, I feel that my family and I have a lot to offer Essie within a safe, loving, permanent home.

We did not know about Essie's situation and only recently found out that she is in state care with a date set for the court to rule. I would have made contact sooner if we had known about her situation. However, it's been two weeks since we (her dad's side of the family) first came to learn of Essie situation. Even though time is of the essence, I'd like to remain hopeful that an assessment appointment can be arranged between us.

We understand Essie will need a great deal of love and support. Transition and change are hard for any child, least of all a six-year-old going through what she has already endured - with so many different placements. I'm personally very close to a foster mum (my friend Hayley Roberts), who has taught me through her journey, how children like Essie needs a little extra love and care.

I am also considerate of both your work commitment and work overload that you will be facing and have faced, dealing with Essie's case this far. But I'd like to plead to your kind nature to allow us the opportunity to share with you all that we, as a family, have to offer.

I am a Community Development Worker and therefore can choose my work hours to take place inside school hours - as I know the importance of having a parent at home. I would like to take this opportunity to explain that I work for The Surrey Gypsy Traveller Communities Forum with the position held of 'Lead in Education', where I am also a committee member.

I believe that Essie would benefit greatly from being placed with us. Not because I am a relative who has had a relationship with her, as we have only met once. She was very young, and it was also a brief encounter. I believe my family and I can enrich her life and provide her with the stability of a family home.

THE MYSTERY IN BEING A GYPSY

Please rest assured that we do value education, contrary to negative stereotypes that can be believed about our ethnicity when generalising. I have a great relationship with our local Primary School, where both my children attended and where I also worked, for several years, in a trusted position. I would be more than confident with the professionalism of this Primary to give Essie the support that she will need. I also have some experience working with children who have special needs. This includes children with learning difficulties, autism, behavioural and emotional challenges. I would be happy to provide references for my work experience if you wish.

I do hope that we will be considered for an assessment and look forward to hearing back from you as soon as possible, I will leave you with my contact details.

Yours faithfully.

Margaret responded to my email with a telephone call. Her voice was soft and sounded nurturing. It didn't match my idea, of how I imagined she'd sound. She told me that after assessing my sister Sarah she had decided to allow me to take the time slot she had open that was originally booked for Julie. We would be given three hours to be accessed, to be considered for Kinship Care. It normally takes four hours but because Margaret had to travel from Kent to Surrey, she had to compensate for the journey time. We would still need to complete all the paperwork, it just meant we had to get it done promptly.

We conducted the telephone assessment there and then to be ready for the home assessment. Margaret arrived at our home; it was strange that her presence felt familiar to me. I was conscious this could be her first time on a Gypsy caravan site, and that she could be feeling awkward or maybe even a little anxious.

I drew in a calm breath of gratitude that the appearance of our entrance road was welcoming. Margaret didn't come into my home with an ounce of authority (*when I make a reference using 'authority' that's a negative for me*).

I was pleased that after the assessment I had the chance to ask some questions. I needed reassurance to know if we stood a real chance of being considered. My Sarah and I both felt that, in the case of our assessments, Social Services could be just dotting the I's and crossing the T's. We understood that the paperwork had been completed and the order was waiting for approval of the judge. Margaret reassured me that our assessments would be viewed and considered accordingly if we were found to be suitable.

I had a burning question that I found myself wrestling with, throughout the assessment, which repeatedly popped to the forefront of my mind. I needed to ask Margaret about the conversation she had with my Aunt Julie.

When Margaret had finished answering my questions about the order, she then stood up and said she needed to go. At which point I blurted out, a little more abruptly than I had intended, "Margaret, I need to ask you about your conversation you had with my Aunt Julie. When she asked you to consider us, you asked, 'How many more from our side of the family was going to crawl out from the woodwork.' Yet none of us had been contacted to be informed about Essie's situation. Were assumptions made that we wouldn't be interested in taking on the care of Essie, based on our ethnicity?"

Margaret sat back down and confessed that she did say this to my Aunt Julie. She explained that she had been Essie's social worker for quite some time and that since being ready to place a final order, which was set to take place by the end of the month, Essie's father's side of the family had only now come forward. Margaret also shared with me that she had been told that Gypsies consider it shameful to have a child in care, which led her to believe, the only reason Gypsies take responsibility is because they must, not because they want to. I explained that pride and shame certainly weren't our reasons for wanting to be assessed.

I then shared my fears with Margaret of facing prejudice due to stereotypes held about our ethnicity. I further explained that it was important for us to be assessed on what we had to offer Essie as a family.

THE MYSTERY IN BEING A GYPSY

I said, "I'm very well aware of the institutionalised racism within Social Services and I know it's possible that some decision makers own conscious or unconscious bias against my ethnic group and feel we could face discrimination."

Margaret understood this was a real fear of racism for me. Her compassion shown, made me feel comfortable enough to share with her that I believed Essie was part of my spiritual destiny. I explained, I had been feeling as though I had a calling, to care for vulnerable children, way before knowing anything about Essie's situation. How I'd been to three separate meetings where fostering and adoption was brought up without being part of the agenda and how I haven't been able to stop thinking about becoming a foster parent since.

Margaret said, "Genty I have been experiencing goosebumps, whilst you have been talking, and this means something to me spiritually."

At that moment I felt like cuddling Margaret because I'd also been experiencing pleasant electric goosebumps, which gave me a sense of knowing that Margaret was a genuine, honest, and kind soul who I could trust.

Margaret explained that after ending the call with my Aunt Julie, she was completely adamant she would not assess anyone else other than my sister Sarah. But her persistent inner voice kept repeatedly challenging her over the three-day bank holiday weekend. The following Tuesday, she picked up the email I had sent and thought, "What if this family truly has the capacity and all it takes to care for Essie?" And by the time she had finished reading, she had experienced a change of heart.

I then stated, "Even though we have spiritually connected it is important for us to only be considered for the best interests of Essie."

This was important to me, because I was waiting for my own little sign of confirmation: "If Essie should be with our family, it should be for her best interest only". My prayer sent up to God still stood.

Margaret gave her word; she would see to it that any decisions made would be fair and in the best interests of Essie. We continued chatting and I found out Margaret's visit with us, was her first time visiting a site.

So, I asked her, "How were you feeling about having to come on a Gypsy site?"

I assured Margaret, "I'm thick-skinned, and I will not be offended by your reply."

Margaret answered, "I did have reservations about coming as I have had very little experience with Romany-Gypsies and only knew many negative stereotypes."

I said I understood and told Margaret, "There's a lot of negative press in the media and the Gypsy 'mock-a-mentries' on TV are guilty of helping to condition the populous to believe negative stereotypes."

Our assessment lasted four and a half hours, because we ended up chatting so comfortably, we lost sight of the time. I wasn't expecting to hear from Margaret again so soon, but she called me the next day saying, "Hi Genty, sorry I forgot to ask you a question yesterday, and I need the answer to complete the paperwork. Would you consider adopting Essie?"

Unusually for me, I needed no time to think and instinctively replied, "Yes!" Margaret said, "That's all I needed to know, and I am happy to tell you both Sarah and you have passed your assessments."

As soon as the call with Margaret ended, I immediately rang my husband. When he answered, I excitedly blurted out, "Margaret has just called. We passed the assessment and so did my Sarah!"

"I had no doubts Babe," Dan appraisingly replied.

"Dan, I know I should have asked for some time to discuss this with you before giving an answer, but Margaret also asked if we would consider adoption and I told her, we would."

I was pleased with Dan's reassuring reply telling me, "Don't worry we will do whatever it takes to get her."

I then rang my Sarah informing her that we had both passed our assessments. I then asked her, "Did you answer any questions, during your assessment about adoption?"

THE MYSTERY IN BEING A GYPSY

My Sarah said, "No Sis nothing come up about adoption."

I explained what Margaret had said about the 'forgotten' adoption question, and my Sarah replied positively, "Do you know what Sis you're going to get her, I just know it."

I felt my Grandfarver-Nelson would be very proud if he was alive to see that two of his older granddaughters had passed the assessment to be able to take Kinship Care of his great-granddaughter.

I truly have no judgment on what others think, feel, or believe when it comes to faith. I simply feel that when a faith belief is serving a person to be at their best and their belief doesn't impose on or hurt anyone else, then I say, "Each to their own."

I have had enough experiences to know there's something more to our existence than this life here on earth. I feel the residual energy of my loved ones who have passed, and this helps me to become the best version of me that I can be.

My Grandfarver-Nelson would be proud. There wouldn't be many grandfathers who wouldn't be, in this situation. But I didn't just 'think' he would be proud, I knew he was, I felt it spiritually.

11

THE GOAL POST MOVE

Margaret called again, after a week, apologising that when presenting senior Social Services staff with our Kinship Care assessment passes it had made no difference. We were simply not going to be considered, because it had been decided to proceed with the court order.

Social Services had also changed the court order recommendation. They were now applying for an 'adoption' order instead of the 'long-term fostering' order. They had reconsidered to ensure Essie would be given the security of the permanence that an adoption can provide. They were requesting a ruling for 'adoption' only.

Margaret said, "Because you have expressed an interest in adopting, I can contact the adoption team, for you to be assessed, if you'd like me to?"

Hearing this, it was then that I fully understood what Margaret had done. She must have had her suspicions or knew for fact, prior to ringing me about the 'forgotten' adoption question, that her superiors were moving the goal post. A goal post move which would ensure neither my Sarah's family nor mine could have Essie in a Kinship placement. I completely understood, and fully appreciated, that I had a champion in Margaret; just as the Romany-Gypsy families, on Epsom Downs, had a champion in Lady Sybil.

It was crystal clear to me what had taken place. Once Margaret had given her valuable time to assess us, she then presented two assessments that showed both of our families met the Social Services requirements to care for Essie. Even though Essie's mum's side of the family had been given two opportunities to keep Essie with their relatives, her dad's side of the family was not going to be treated the same. Much more importantly, Essie was being denied the opportunity to be placed with us, where she would receive all the love, care, and attention that she deserved within a Kinship placement.

Margaret said, "Genty if you and Dan decide to go the adoption route, the first step would be to allocate you an Adoption Social Worker."

I was deflated, feeling that it would be a fruitless task to take the adoption route having our ethnicity against us.

I asked Margaret, "Is it at least possible to be allocated with someone who has had previous experience working with our ethnic community, and who are familiar with visiting on a site?"

I didn't want to have win over or educate, in this situation, those who are apprehensive of my ethnicity before my family and me would be considered for who we are. It was the only thing I could think of saying. I felt as though I was clutching at straws because I knew very well it would only take a single person within the adoption process to hold a bias, which could then result in us failing to become registered adopters.

Margaret understood and said, "I will make some inquiries and get back to you."

Dan and I discussed the commitment, time, cost, and challenges that becoming adopters would demand. We decided to go for it, feeling our impediments were worth taking the chance on because if we didn't try, it was a definite that we wouldn't get Essie.

I was feeling devastated, my heart felt like it had sunk into my stomach. It was 'agreed' by the professional decision-makers, in charge of Essie's case, that they would apply for a long-term fostering order.

These Social Services staff members had already automatically assumed that our side of the family did not want to be assessed for Kinship Care. And now, after we had approached them, pleaded with them, got an assessment, and passed - Social Services had suddenly reconsidered and changed their decision regarding 'what' was in Essie's best interest.

There was no such order, for adoption, that had been considered by these professionals (to ensure the stability and the permanency an adoption can provide) before my Sarah, and I had passed our assessments.

My mind raced, looking at the road ahead. I wished I had never shared my passion 'on record' to foster because there was a better possibility for us to foster Essie, than there was to adopt her. I felt if I hadn't had shared, what I believed to be a part of my spiritual journey - to 'care for children in need' by becoming a foster parent - then the order would have remained a long-term fostering one.

I spoke to God in my mind, I felt that God had laid it on my heart to consider fostering to be ready for Essie.

"God, if this is your plan, then guide me to the open doors that I may not see yet. God, the goal post has been moved overnight. It feels like a direct sabotage! Guide and protect us in righteousness, Amen."

It felt so frustrating to once again contemplate that what had taken place was racism. Based on nothing more than the Social Services staffs bigoted behaviour.

Yet, when I'm subjected to such unjust behaviour this evokes an ancestral warrior spirit within, and it's a mighty one.

If they had moved the goal posts due to their bias held, then it was time to fight against it.

I mentally promised my Grandfarver- Nelson that we'd do everything we could to get Essie, and I found myself craving the encouragement cuddle I knew my Dad would have wrapped me in, if he were here.

An appointment, for our Adoption Social Worker (Janet), to visit had been arranged. Janet needed to write up the recommendation for stage-two of the adoption process. I was pleased Margaret came too, because I felt no connection or familiarity with Janet, who whilst completing the relevant paperwork, told us several times: I need to make you aware when adopting this means you receive no financial help for Essie.

The adoption assessment took four and a half hours to complete, and Janet had managed to irritate me as many times, as she felt the need to remind us, we wouldn't receive any financial support.

THE MYSTERY IN BEING A GYPSY

She was interested to know if I had had a wedding, like the ones shown on the TV programme, 'My Big Fat Gypsy Wedding'.

I curtly replied, "No" and asked, "Have you ever worked with any English Romany-Gypsies, or been on a site before?"

Janet proclaimed, "I have had loads of experience."

But from the questions she asked, I had mentally doubted her honesty and I felt we were the first Romany-Gypsy family she had known, because 'My Big Fat Gypsy Wedding' was a sensationalised channel 4 series predominantly about Irish Travellers.

If Janet would have had any experience, she would have at least known the difference between English Romany-Gypsies and an Irish Travellers. For a start, if nothing else, our accents are a great indication that we are not Irish.

Janet also stated, "I am aware there is a high level of domestic abuse among Travellers," as though in some way to prove her expertise and knowledge of Travellers.

Considering how she'd just made a sweeping generalisation that wasn't true, I was pleased to have on hand the evidence to correct her. I explained to Janet that I had recently attended a Domestic Abuse (DA) conference. My friend Louisa had held the position of 'Lead in DA' for the SGTCF at that time and had been invited to attend; I was Louisa's 'plus one'. We heard so many harrowing stories of abuse that only a person with a heart of stone would have been able to listen to them without crying. A speaker at this conference shared their findings that led her to believe, higher levels of DA seem to occur among women whose partners have high profile and demanding jobs. I highlighted this information share to Janet that the speaker was talking about the men from her ethnicity, not mine.

I knew my frustration had shown in my tone and reply. I had gotten up to get the flyer from the DA conference (which evidenced that I had attended) and took the opportunity, out of Janets eyesight, to control my breathing. I then handed the leaflet to Janet and sat back down next to Dan, he gave me a discreet nudge on my leg and without him using words I knew he was reminding me, "Steady, tread carefully."

When our meeting had finished, Janet asked, "Can we walk around the site to take look?" Margaret looked slightly uncomfortable with Janet's request and reminded her of the time.

But Janet was obviously not at all concerned with time - replying, "Oh it will only take a few minutes I just want to look around the site, maybe we can meet some others."

I was so pleased when Dan replied, "I wouldn't be able to walk you around the site to meet our neighbours' we didn't know this was part of the adoption process. If we did, I could have planned with our neighbours', for them to meet with you."

I was relieved when they left, because the pressure I felt to defend my own ethnic group, and challenge Janet's 'Gypsy expertise', (which ordinarily I would have done so robustly), was immense. She had left my home without me educating or correcting her beliefs, which had clearly been based on watching a Channel 4 TV Show, because I couldn't take the chance of 'offending' her. After we waved them off, I closed the door and turned to Dan to get a much-needed cuddle. I confessed to him I found it hard to tolerate Janet's negative stereotyping. Dan reminded me it isn't my responsibility to educate the world; it's simply, in this situation, to show all we have to offer Essie.

We received a letter saying our 'Registration of Interest' had been accepted by Kent County Council (KCC) Adoption Service. We had now officially begun our adoption journey. The next steps were for us to provide character references, get our Disclosure and Barring Service (DBS) forms completed, paid for, and sent off (the DBSs were needed to prove no member of my family has a criminal recorded).

Also, we had to pay for our health assessments and then send all the requested documents to KCC at speed. There were mountains of paperwork for us to complete online. Margaret had clearly pulled some strings for us to be fast-tracked through the adoption process, but it was made clear to us (by Janet) that we could complete the course work, be approved as adopters, but at the end of it all we still might not be matched with Essie.

THE MYSTERY IN BEING A GYPSY

After seven intense months of completing the training courses, being approved as financially stable, mentally sound-of-mind, physically healthy and non-criminals, we now had the adoption panel to face. My anxiety of having to face the adoption panel, where all eyes would be firmly judging us, made me feel physically sick. During this time, I hated the fact our ethnicity was known. We drove down to Kent, making sure we allowed enough spare time for any M25 traffic, (the M25 is a heavy traffic motorway which can have unexpected delays).

We met with Margaret and Janet fifteen minutes before we were scheduled to face the panel. This was one of the last two hurdles yet to be jumped before we could become approved adopters. Janet reminded us that the panel of people we would be meeting today have the control. It didn't make any difference how much time, money, energy, and commitment we had shown already to have Essie join our family; all that mattered in the here and now was what this panel of people thought and then decided.

An adoption panel is made up of adoptive parents, people who have been adopted, a chairperson, a minute-taker, and an independent panel adviser.

We walked through the building and took a seat outside the panel meeting room. I took the opportunity to sit in silence, concentrating on my breathing to help steady my nerves (anxiety). All I wanted and prayed for, was for us to be judged as individuals, and not by any conscious or unconscious bias, those sitting on the panel, may hold against our ethnicity. As ever, I was pleased to have Dan take over the small talk that does help to pass the time when waiting. Unfortunately, it's not an ability I have, and I prefer to sit in silence to collect my thoughts. I looked up at the small window above us and just as I did a little robin perched itself on the windowsill. This gave me comfort because I took it to be a spiritual sign of good news.

I believed I had done a good job of steadying my nerves, but once it was time to go into the meeting room to face the panel, when I stood up, I suddenly felt sick again. I was using my inner voice to tell myself, "Don't be sick," on a repeated mantra. And yet, we didn't receive the interrogation I had feared we would be subjected to, and it was a pleasant surprise not to be asked a single question about any of the TV 'mock-a-mentries' that air about our ethnicity under the term Traveller or the word Gypsy. It was quite the opposite of what my anxiety had fearfully been imaging.

A lady on the panel said, "I would have loved to have had more time to talk with you about your work and being invited to attend events which are held in Westminster."

Confession time: Yes, I did include this information to impress! In the hope that this would help me to be viewed as an individual, and for the person I am. I strongly believe this information sharing helped, in some way, to earn the positive recommendation of the panel, which was given to us by a unanimous decision. I cried as I thanked each one of them individually and then fell into Dan arms where we held each other tightly, forgetting for just a moment where we were.

We went on to be matched with Essie, but not before our final meeting, where we had been presented with a brochure about children needing and waiting to be adopted. I was completely overwhelmed and wished I could take them all. Even though we were adopting Essie, I took the time to read the insert description next to each of the photos of the children being advertised.

I hadn't noticed I was hyper-ventilating until Dan told me, "Slow your breathing."

My heart told me, "I could love and care for them all." My head told me, "It's impossible!"

The next step was to meet with Essie's foster carers. A date was offered to us via an email from Margaret, which fell on a day that Dan had work commitments he couldn't get out of.

So, I rang Margaret to explain asking, "Should we try to reschedule or go ahead without Dan?"

We decided to go ahead with the date offered, respecting it was convenient for Essie's foster carers Duncan, and Kay.

I asked Louisa if she would like to come with me and even though she understood that she may have needed to sit in the car,

THE MYSTERY IN BEING A GYPSY

whilst I met with the foster carers, she was delighted that I had asked her. This meeting was to have the opportunity to learn all we could about Essie from Duncan and Kay. I wanted to know as much as possible and requested if Margaret could also arrange a meeting with Essie's schoolteacher. After all, a teacher can have a valuable perception, because they can give their views through a less emotional attachment. I've come to learn that some emotions can be responsible for clouding judgments, and I was pleased to have confirmation that after our meeting with Duncan and Kay, we'd then be able to go to Essie's school to meet with her teacher.

I picked Louisa up and we then drove for over an hour to get to the destination in Kent. I was feeling a little nervous and quite excited. This was going to be a step closer to learning all about Essie. Duncan and Kay had now taken care of Essie for nearly a year, and I couldn't wait to hear all they had to tell me. I intended to do my best to give them a good first impression of me. Margaret had informed me foster carers are allowed to have their opinion known, regarding their thoughts and feelings, of the suitability of the family that is needed for the child they are fostering.

Louisa and I arrived twenty minutes early as I much prefer to be early than on time. Margaret was standing outside the building, with her work colleague, waiting to meet us. She was wearing her infectious smile and looked as happy and excited as I felt. Her colleague kindly offered both Louisa and I in for a coffee. Lousia was excitedly chatting away with Margaret and her colleague in the kitchen area, and it was nice for me to have some spare time alone to collect my thoughts.

I walked into the small room, which was usually in use for supervised visits, for parents to meet with their children who have been taken into state care. I noticed some toys, suitable for babies and toddlers in one corner. The seating area was arranged in a semi-circle and there was a large double door that opened onto a garden which was well kept with freshly cut grass. Tall trees served as a boundary perimeter that provided privacy for the garden.

I took a seat and very quickly allowed myself to sink into the comfort of the armchair. It was a beautiful bright day which provided me with my most perfect preferred weather that always reminds me of my Dad. I love the days that start with a crisp cool morning that turns into a warm, bright, cloud-free day and so did my Dad. You know those days that neither require a coat for warmth, nor summer clothes for comfort. It's in life's most beautiful moments, and also my most anxious times that I find myself thinking or yearning for my Dad the most. Just looking outside at 'our' perfect weather made a smile curl up at the sides of my mouth. I could feel his proudness and I also felt pleased, having overcome so many hurdles to be seated in this position, I was soaking up the reality that Essie will soon be our daughter.

Louisa, Margaret, and her colleague joined me, taking their seats in the room. Margaret said, "Janet has called to let us know she is running behind and that we should start our meeting without her, and she will join us as soon as she can."

About ten minutes later Duncan flounced into the room with his wife Kay following behind. I stood up and walked over to greet them. Without giving me a second glance Duncan asked Margaret if he could have a word before the meeting started.

Their sheer presence had managed to change the ambience in the room and the pleasant feeling I had just moments before their arrival suddenly disappeared.

Margaret responded that it would be fine for Duncan to have a word, and then acknowledged my presence with introductions. I made an apology for my husband's absence and explained he had work commitments. I very quickly followed on to further explain that my friend Louisa, had accompanied me on my journey but wasn't going to be a part of our scheduled meeting. I felt the need to share this with them, as Duncan seemed a little agitated, maybe even aggravated.

He gave me a nod in response and Kay politely replied, "Oh that's fine." Duncan again reasserted his need to have a word with Margaret and added that this should be done in private. With an air of importance, he turned and walked out of the room and Kay went

THE MYSTERY IN BEING A GYPSY

with him. Margaret shot me a look that needed no words, she instantly flushed red and left the room to follow them behind.

I felt somewhat unhappy at their lack of an apology for being late, more so due to the fact this meeting was after all taking place locally to them. Their late arrival and need to leave just as soon as they had arrived to have a 'private word', was a perfect combination which had given me a bad first impression of them.

I turned to Louisa and rokkered, "Mandi gins foki no kush". Louisa shot me that look, one I'd seen many times over the years, I knew she was once again surprised at my quick verdict and was not in agreement with it either.

Louisa was in her element. She was very pleased to be with me and consciously she held a view that all foster carers are the world's kindest people. Personally, I'm not as easily worshipping of people. I am not one to generalise that all can be the same, and my preference is to not generalise at all wherever possible.

They didn't stay outside the room long and by the time they'd returned Louisa had already gone next door and was keeping company with Margaret's colleague; I was pleased she didn't have to wait in the car.

Janet had also arrived by this time and came into the room just in front of Margaret, who didn't now seem her bubbly self and I noticed she had developed bright red hives on her neck.

Margaret and Janet sat to my right on two spare chairs. Duncan and Kay sat directly opposite me on the sofa, and I took the armchair chair I had been relaxing in earlier. Margaret started the meeting by asking Duncan and Kay to tell me about Essie. I couldn't help but wonder what had gone on outside the room, because whatever it was it had noticeably effected Margaret. I toyed with the idea of asking Duncan if what he needed to have a word about had been sufficiently answered. I had a sense of 'knowing' it was something about me personally. The only thing that stopped me was my nervous inner voice that reminded me, yet again, "I was the one being judged."

However, I did come to learn what Duncan's urgent question was later in the day.

Kay spoke first and reeled off in a 'bullet point style' what she chose to share with me. She told me that since Essie had been with them, she could now use the cutlery correctly, she has a good sleeping routine and goes to bed at 7:30 every night and sleeps until 7 in the morning. She said Essie's ability to spell and read had taken a clear leapfrog in the right direction. Kay bragged that her forte and passion was being able to get Essie to read and write well. She said Essie's handwriting was appalling and that she had no pride in writing whatsoever. Essie was in two different after-school clubs and also took swimming lessons once a week.

I asked if they had any children of their own and learned that they had a teenage daughter called Angelia. Kay at this point went on to explain how hard it had been on her daughter because Essie would enter Angelia's bedroom without permission and constantly gave Angelia jibes.

Kay asserted, "Essie has the ability and capability to make Angelia feel very uncomfortable."

Duncan took over and seemed to enjoy (way too much, for my liking) telling me,

"When Essie is naughty and is corrected, she throws out of control tantrums that can last between 20-30 minutes."

For the most part I had just been listening and giving the occasional nod to show I was engaged. But what they were telling me now, instinctively prompted me to interrupt Duncan to ask, "Can you tell me more about the behaviours of Essie's tantrums?"

Duncan shifted his position to rest his right foot on his left knee. He then used his hand as if to wipe something forcibly from his mouth. He drew in an exaggerated breath and proceeded to set the scene of this little six-year-old girl who throws a tantrum with or without cause.

He stated, "Essie throws tantrums in her room, after we place her there for being naughty. We close the door leaving her to it, she can do a lot of screaming or crying, but she can also be violent."

I asked him could he elaborate on the violent behaviour and Duncan replied, "She throws things around, punches and kicks the door in her room. But she has also done this to the other doors in our home."

I'm not sure what else got said in the next few minutes, because my thought process kicked in as I contemplated if this little girl's hurt, pain, and fear was being played out in what looked like, to Duncan and Kay, to be naughty behaviour and throwing tantrums. I was struggling to understand why a child who had been placed in foster care, who had suffered, would be disciplined by isolation. My thoughts managed to evoke the emotion of sadness and the tears that stung my eyes brought me immediately back into my surroundings. Having raised two children of my own, and spending most of my time in the company of children, this information had caused a tightening in the pit of my stomach thinking about this child being left alone in such emotional despair.

When the sting of tears which watered my eyes, had helped me to return to the present moment, Kay was saying, "Essie's bad behaviour could really be quite menacing."

Maybe my blank facial expression and watery eyes had prompted Kay to 'enforce' their point about how naughty and deserving of solitary confinement Essie was.

Kay continued, "Essie can be really snipey and its just awful when she gets on Angelia's case." It was clear to see that this snipey behaviour was a big problem for Kay, when she applied hand actions of "Chatter, Chatter, Chatter", (used normally when singing the song 'The Wheels on a Bus Go Round and Round' to toddlers), to empathize the word 'snipey'. Angelia is around the same age to our daughter, and I felt it was important to get a better understanding of Essie and Angelia's relationship.

I listened to Kay tell me all about how Angelia feels, but I had not yet heard an example of what this 'snipey behaviour' was, and I had never heard of this word before.

So, after being as polite as I could by listening all about Angelia, I again interrupted to ask Kay if she could give me an example of what snipey is.

Kay said, "I can give you an example of this snipey behaviour that happened just the other day. We were out on a car journey and Essie, out of nowhere, had just decided to stare at Angelia. I will admit this doesn't sound much but being poor Angelia on the receiving end of these long periods of time, when Essie is just sat staring relentlessly at her, it is just awful. Her menacing staring can make you feel really uncomfortable."

Kay then continued by giving another example of being snipey, which was when Essie had told Angelia, "Kay loves me best because she opens my door and helps me out of the car, but she doesn't help you."

Hearing this, I couldn't help but wonder if Essie and Angelia were being treated differently. No sooner had Kay finished this example of being 'snipey' Duncan recalled the time when Essie had propositioned them both, asking them to choose either Angelia or her to be their daughter.

I felt my shoulders release the tension I had been holding, while awaiting the information that would challenge me into doubting if I would be able to handle Essie's behaviour. But instead, hearing this information, I had to do my best not to laugh at Essie's intellect to own propositioning skills at the age of six.

Margaret then awkwardly announced, "Genty, Essie refers to her dad's side of the family as pikeys and we are working with her to correct this terminology, hopefully we can achieve this before she joins your family."

It was clear Margaret understood the word pikey is a derogatory slur used to insult Gypsies. I gave the information no energy by simply replying, "It's no problem we're thick-skinned, Essie is a child, and most children simply repeat language that's used around them."

Duncan sought the opportunity to clarify, "She wouldn't have picked up such a word from us." He then went on to share another story:

THE MYSTERY IN BEING A GYPSY

"Once, when we were going out in our car, we noticed Travellers had pitched up in our local field. Essie instantly became animated and angry upon spotting them. She wanted to know, 'Why don't the police do anything about 'those' Gypsies?' And she asked me, 'Why don't the police just remove them off our land?'"

Duncan confessed, "I just didn't know how to answer her because after all, it is typical, and wrong what the Gypsies do."

Hearing Duncan's fast talking, bordering on ramblings, of his version of this event helped confirm my first impression: these people held conscious bias against me due to my ethnicity.

For me Duncan is a prime example of those extremely ignorant people who generalise, stereotype and who would most certainly be capable of racial discrimination. His storytelling had told me all I needed to know about his thinking and beliefs about Romany-Gypsies in general. I wondered what terms he may use when speaking about my ethnic group, when not in my presents or that of the social workers.

Duncan looked quite comfortable and seemed to be in his element, having all eyes on him; and without pausing for breath rolled into another story telling opportunity:

"Last Christmas we went to a family dinner. We were sitting around the table, and I was talking about a dog we used to own, not the dog we have now. His name was Roger and all of a sudden and out of nowhere Essie burst into tears and screamed, 'Stop Talking About My Dad!' At first, I had no idea why she was so upset, I mean just because the dog had the same name as her dad, I couldn't see why she thought I was talking badly about him - I was talking about the dog, the dog we owned before Essie had arrived."

Not one of us responded to Duncan's story. Least of all did any of us sympathise with him that he couldn't understand why Essie felt as though Ducan had been sitting around the dinner table 'on Christmas day' speaking badly of her dad. An awkward moment of silence followed.

A pattern had emerged with Duncan's storytelling. His need to reassure me, and to defend himself, whilst asserting his lack of ability to understand Essie. He felt the need to tell me he wasn't a racist person, and that Essie didn't learn the word pikey from being in their family. He painted a picture that Essie, the six-year-old, allegedly has her own mindset about Romany-Gypsies that just so happened to align with the bigoted reports to be found in The Sun and the Daily Mail newspapers regularly: that Travellers have no rights to pull on any land, anywhere.

Margaret broke the silence by saying, "I am conscious of the time, we should be getting ready to go to our next appointment, I am afraid we are running a behind. Genty, is there anything else you would like to ask before we go?"

I smiled at Margaret and shook my head, "No."

Kay then informed me, "Essie's clothes will be neatly packed and sent in a suitcase, as I'm a very orderly person in such ways."

I gave her a nod whilst telling her, "They will be gratefully received as I am also a very orderly person, who prides myself on keeping an orderly and hygienically clean home."

Confession time again! I shared my cleanliness standard due to being cautious to whether Duncan and Kay, are indeed the type of people who believe Gypsies are dirty; just as those playground mothers, who were challenged by Mum to a cleaning inspection believed. But in due course we would all be visiting each other's homes, and they would then see with their own eyes my cleanliness standard and I would see there's. If they did believe this stereotype, it would soon enough be dispelled.

Janet asked Kay and Duncan if they had any final questions for me, and Duncan replied, "Nope. You're the professional I trust you have already asked all the questions needed."

I drew in a long-controlled breath that gave me just enough composure and decorum to thank them for their time given. Then formal goodbyes between us all were exchanged, and Duncan and Kay left promptly thereafter.

12

THE SWORD USED AS A SHIELD

There was little time for reflection, as we needed to make our way over to the school to meet Essie's teacher, knowing even before we left that we'd probably arrive late. When we did arrive late, the headteacher greeted us without having any problem, stressing the importance of her time. She asserted the obvious when stating, "I agreed to a twenty-minute appointment, and you are nearly ten minutes late!"

Her tone of voice was familiar to me, as one of a professional in 'authority'.

She said curtly, "There isn't enough time for the meeting to now take place."

Margaret handled the head teacher's brusqueness well, by apologising and explaining the long distance I'd travelled and that we had just previously met the foster carers who had arrived late, which had helped to put us behind.

Margret then requested, "If we could take advantage of the ten minutes left?" And expressed the importance for me to have some knowledge of Essie's academic skills.

Thankfully, the headteacher softened and Margaret managed to get our 20-minute meeting rescheduled. I was ecstatic to have the opportunity to hear another viewpoint about Essie. I now just needed to wait an hour to hear more.

Janet, Margaret, Louisa, and I walked to a small row of shops, where each of us bought some food for lunch. The weather was still nice, so we took a seat in the nearby park. Louisa was just bursting to know all I'd found out about Essie and said, "Please will you tell me about her now." She had already asked me, during our car journey to make our way over to the school, but I was following Margaret on roads I didn't know and needed to concentrate on driving. And that was the only reason I hadn't already told her everything that was said in the meeting.

I began to tell Louisa, "Essie understandably has some behavioural issues." Our conversation was cut short when Janet interrupted telling us, "Essie's case is confidential, she is a LAC (Looked After Child), and we shouldn't be speaking about her."

I rolled my eyes to Louisa, not really caring if Janet saw me, and then laid back and relaxed on the grass. I was still winding down from the tensions my body held as a result of meeting Essie's foster carers. Mother nature's soothing grass blanket and the placid warmth of the sun were beginning to do the job nicely. However, it was short-lived because my thinking mind awoke, to remind me about Duncan's private word he needed to have with Margaret.

I gave in, sat up, and asked, "Margaret what was Duncan's question he needed to ask?" She responded with an apology, "I am sorry Genty it was quite unprofessional of them to behave as they did."

My response was to assure Margaret, "You do not need to apologise to me on their behalf." Margaret shared with us that Duncan explained to her, he hadn't realised the relatives who were taking the adoption forward were from the dad's side of the family. His shock of finding this out, on the morning of our meeting, had posed a problem for Duncan and he needed to ask Margaret, "How do you talk to her? We have never spoken with a Gypsy before."

Louisa gasped at hearing this, but I had no reaction because I wasn't at all surprised. I appreciated hearing that Margaret had replied to Duncan, "You should speak, in the same way, tone and manner that you would speak to anyone else!" She then informed them that our meeting needed to start.

Poor Margaret, she looked mortified and apologetically confessed she felt she had let me down and should have simply told him, "They were late and that our meeting needed to start, and that he could ask questions after."

I again assured Margaret that she shouldn't worry herself over it. But it was more than obvious Duncan's attitude had made Margaret somehow feel responsible, though from my point of view, she wasn't responsible at all. We sat in silence for a little while until a thought popped into my mind that I shared by asking, "Do you think it would be a good idea to offer Duncan and Kay the opportunity to visit our home, prior to them bringing Essie to us for the introduction process?" I went on to explain, "I believe it would be an opportunity for them to deal with their own inhibitions, and my family would make them more than welcome."

Margaret replied, "That is a very kind gesture Genty, and certainly something for us to think about."

We walked back to the school, arriving five minutes early. I heard from Essie's teacher that she is a sociable little girl and was informed she tries hard to form friendships and to academically meet her targets. After leaving the school I could not wait to get home to share everything about the day's events with Dan. On the drive home I told Louisa 'everything' that had gone on in the meeting with Duncan and Kay. Louisa allowed me to vent, then agreed that my first impression was correct!

When I arrived home Dan made me a coffee and we sat down to chat. He wrapped his arms around me as I off-loaded how Duncan was another of those people who generalise, stereotype, and holds a bias attitude towards us. Dan knew I had once again found myself in a position I struggled immensely in; one where every inch of my being wants to challenge anti-ethnic bias but against my instinct and authenticity, I had had to remain silent. We decided to get an early night and agreed to speak about the 'Duncan situation' again in the morning.

I woke up feeling even more uneasy about Duncan's attitude. I was worried about his ability to visit our home during the process of introductions, without projecting his bias, about our ethnicity, onto Essie. I am a great believer in 'energies', and I know how brilliantly children can pick up on authentic feelings. My years spent in the company of children has evidenced it. After speaking again with Dan, we both agreed I should write an email to Margaret and Janet offering our invitation to Duncan and Kay formally. We also wanted to know if Essie was receiving any professional help with her behaviour.

Dear Margaret and Janet,

After our meeting on the 20th of July 2016, where I shared an idea to offer an invitation for Duncan and Kay to visit our home, Dan and I have now discussed this, and we feel an invite should be offered. We believe their pre-visit without Essie will be beneficial to help ensure Essie will experience a positive introduction process.

What seems to be present are some barriers which exist due to negative stereotypes in relation to our ethnicity. Taking into consideration Duncan didn't know how to speak with a Gypsy, this leads us to believe he will struggle with having to come on a site where 15 other Romany-Gypsy families also live.

Hearing that Essie was demanding to know, "Why the police weren't arresting the Gypsies to remove them from 'her' land?" This for us, is a clear indication that Essie has had the divide of 'othering' taught to her. Furthermore, Duncan shared with us that Essie becomes angry and animated when she 'spots' caravans. Many residents where we live own caravans, and it will be inevitable that Essie will see them when she arrives.

Essie deserves for us, as the adults involved during her fast-tracked introduction, to be committed, and dedicated to conducting this process by ensuring she feels safe and happy.

Essie was described as, "Good when she is good and when horrible she has violent outbursts of crying, screaming, shouting, punching, and kicking." These behaviours, described as having tantrums, can last up to half an hour and can present several times a day. Having had the time to reflect upon this information, we feel there is a possibility her behaviours point to a little girl

THE MYSTERY IN BEING A GYPSY

who is possibly suffering from behavioural issues and/or a disorder. Due to the difficulties Essie has endured having multiple caregivers and facing the uncertainty of her own future, we wish to understand if Essie has been diagnosed with any disorders.

Even though the offer had been made and it was truly intended for the best interests of Essie; Duncan and Kay declined our offer to visit us at home on our site. It was certainly a missed opportunity for them to learn much more than they knew about us, and more importantly as the soon-to-be adoptive parents of Essie.

I would have been happy to have found some common ground with Essie's foster carers. We had three months until the introduction process would take place and I honestly felt we could have used this time to get to know each other and (who knows) we could have even formed some sort of friendship as stranger things have happened. But they replied to Margaret informing her that they would not 'need' a pre-visit, prior to bringing Essie to our home, because "they knew how to conduct themselves professionally."

I personally held anxious reservations; I had already witnessed their 'professionalism' at our first meeting and couldn't imagine how Duncan would be capable of handling coming onto a site, where all the residents were Romany-Gypsies, when he needed to be advised on, how to speak with a Gypsy in the first place.

Margaret informed us that Essie did not have any diagnoses noted in her files and that she had not seen a professional to be assessed, which also meant she hadn't received any additional support either. We learned from Essie's files that her aunt (her mum's sister who I will call aunt-L) had helped with her care since was she born. So, Dan and I decided it would be a good idea to reach out to aunt-L.

We knew through Margaret that aunt-L resented us for going forward with the adoption and she had made it clear she didn't like us, even though we had never met. But that didn't matter to us one bit. What did matter, was that aunt-L would know what Essie's normal behaviours were. I asked Margaret to contact aunt-L to find out if she would speak with me, because what she knew about our soon-to-be daughter would be of paramount importance.

On the 22nd of September 2016, Margaret emailed to suggest that we make a video, filming a tour around our home and surroundings. The purpose was to help make Essie's new home familiar to her before arriving. She suggested buying a soft toy and placing it in every room whilst asking, "Can see the toy, Essie?" In a 'Where's Wally' type game. Knowing Essie loves horses, we'd bought a soft toy horse. We completed the video and wrote a letter to Essie introducing ourselves and sent it to Duncan and Kay's address.

I had to attend one last meeting in Kent about Essie. The lady who chaired the meeting asked lots of questions of Kay, that was in the form of a checklist:

How well is Essie doing in school?

Is Essie up to date with her immunisations?

Optician appointments up to date?

Dental appointments up to date?

Is there any progress being made with the urinary incontinence?

Kay replied, "Essie has gotten used to wearing pull-ups and this works well for us because I just can't go back to those days, I feel too old to be getting up in the night dealing with wet sheets." Kay added, "We are sure Essie isn't wetting herself during the night but when she wakes in the morning, she is choosing not to use the toilet."

My first thoughts were for Essie, I wondered how it would feel for her, coming to yet another new family, especially with a bedwetting problem. It wasn't the first time, I was sat listening amazed at what was being said between professional, educated, and trained people in authority. Because they just accepted the information. No further questions followed.

THE MYSTERY IN BEING A GYPSY

Surely bed-wetting for a now seven-year-old, who'd faced the struggles Essie had was an Alert 101? And why hadn't I learned about this before now?

Why had none of these so-called professionals ever thought to arrange an assessment for her?

Because I certainly couldn't have Kay's attitude towards this child, even though we are close to being the same age.

I didn't see any point in asking questioning, nor was I given the opportunity to do so. I was there as a guest, to simply listen about Essie. But hearing this new information, I didn't feel confident that just because Essie didn't have any disorders, emotional or behavioural problems noted in her file, that this did not mean she didn't have any.

I was not feeling assured enough to just 'Trust the Professionals'.

13

SIX DAYS

The 13th of October 2016 was our scheduled date to meet Essie for the first time, and the beginning of the 'six-day' introduction process. Our request to have the longest introduction process possible had been denied. It had been decided, by the professionals, and agreed by the foster carers, that Essie's introductions process would be completed from 'start to finish' within six days. We found ourselves in a situation that we were not happy with, because we felt it would be better for Essie to have more time to get to know us. But it was out of our control. We just had to do our very best to bring our ace game out for the next six days and then for the rest of our lives as Essie's parents.

I can see how such short introduction time frames work well for much younger children, and for their adoptive parents, for Social Services, the social workers, and the foster carers. But our case was a little different considering Essie was now seven years old. Six days for the 'transitioning process introductions' to support her into her new family and home that she had no choice about in the matter was, 'unnecessarily' rushed, from our point of view. Especially when taking into consideration that the planning in this process hadn't made any provisions for Essie to stay with us overnight at any point during the six days. I was concerned this move could be the one that rocked her world. When the cup is already full it only takes a single droplet that results in the spill over.

Day 1: Dan and I had found Duncan and Kay's home address with little effort, thanks to the help of the Sat-Nav. We parked around the corner from their home, simply because it felt like a less intrusive place to park. I stepped outside and sucked in a long, slow breath of the cool October, 10 am morning. I was attentive to Dan because this was his first time meeting the foster carers. I got out my phone and sent Kay a text letting her know we had arrived.

Dan took my hand and asked, "You ready?" I gave him a nod and we walked down their road. Dan had a firm grip on my hand and walked slightly in front, leading the way. Just before reaching their front door, Dan fell back to the position of Second In Command.

He gestured with his hand, you lead the way, and said with a smile, "After you."

Just as soon as I'd pressed the doorbell Kay greeted us with a dramatic, "Hello."

She was holding Essie in one arm; in the typical and practical way all mums seem to do instinctively. And there she was, 'our' Essie! Her arms were wrapped tightly around Kay's neck with her head laying on her shoulder, her hair served as a covering which ensured we couldn't see her face. Kay stood her on the floor and Essie took the opportunity to glance up at us. I was just as quick with my response, crouching down to her level to offer her the toy-horse. Essie held out her hand to receive the gift, and I then completely understood the relevance and importance of the 'Where's Wally' video and gift.

We were invited into their living room and took our seats. Kay directed Essie through conversation, preparation, (and a small amount of bribery) to interact with us. This beautiful little girl, who I was totally smitten with at first glance, didn't show any further signs of being embarrassed. It was strange to think, in just six days, Essie would become our daughter for the rest of our lives. Watching her offer my husband his choice of some cupcakes was so surreal.

Essie seemed very pleased with Dan's choice. She walked over and offered me a cupcake, and my choice also seemed to please her. Neither Dan nor I knew that Essie was fixated on getting the 'single' chocolate cupcake for herself. I'm sure it could have been a very different beginning to our story if either of us had chosen the chocolate cupcake Essie wanted!

I watched her through eyes of forgiveness and hope, that the adoption prep groups, and training days had taught us to understand.

These groups, that we had the privilege to attend, about understanding possible behaviours we may encounter with children who have spent time in state care. It was all now about to play out.

Being in Duncan and Kay's home, for less than ten minutes, it became obvious they were strict on rules. Essie had gotten out a tiny coffee table, which suited her size perfectly, and placed her cupcake on it. She then darted off into the kitchen and returned with a beaker of water, which she stood down next to her cupcake. No sooner had she done so than Duncan got a coaster, placed it under her beaker and in a firm tone said,

"That's not what we do here, is it Essie?" She paid little attention, giving Duncan no response.

Essie's focus was solely blinkered on her cupcake. I watched her eat: one bite, two chews, a gulping swallow, at a pace many adults would not be able to manage without choking. Kay announced that Essie had done a wonderful job in choosing the cakes, telling us that she was given the choice to choose on our behalf. I complimented Essie on how great the cupcakes tasted; I am not sure she heard me because she was in a trance-like state whilst eating and didn't respond.

Essie had finished her cupcake by the time I had managed half of mine. Kay then asked her to get her leaver's book to show it to us. It contained well wishes and photos from her class friends and teachers. The school had made a great effort for Essie and had gifted her a beautiful silver necklace with a little cross attached. Essie placed the book on my lap, I opened the book, and she took over, to turn the pages quickly. She then closed the book and left the room to go upstairs, returning with a nail varnish play kit and an offer to paint my nails.

This engagement was more than I'd dared to dream of for our first meeting. Watching Essie slowly and very accurately paint my nails, I was engrossed. The organic connection I felt, I hoped that Essie could feel it too.

Human interaction is a fascinating thing. With both my own children I'd assumed the love and instant protective instinct was because I had brought them into the world, but right now, Essie had

THE MYSTERY IN BEING A GYPSY

unknowingly stolen my heart. When my nails were finished, Essie asked if I'd like to have a tattoo and had already grabbed a tiny sheet of paper that had a few different designs on it. Her movements were so quick. She asked me to choose one and I in return asked her to choose for me. She put the tattoo paper onto the back of my hand and used a wet wipe to unstick the paper from the tattoo. Pulling the paper off revealed her chosen design, it was a tiny pink heart. I spiritually took this to be a sign - of confirmation that Essie had given me a tiny piece of her heart - in exchange for stealing mine.

Essie clearly understood this meeting was for her to find out as much as she could about us, she challenged both Dan and I through her leading of play, taking complete control. I felt this little girl's spirit had not been broken, at some point during her short life she had decided to fight.

The games we played created a lot of laughter for us all. Tickling Essie, playing sleeping lions, then jumping up and down obeying Essie's concession of commands, including her exercise instructions given, going from plank to star jumps and then playing hopscotch which had gotten me out of breath. But Dan and I were literally lost in those moments of engaging with her. Essie once again changed the game. Standing up on the armchair she told me to give her a piggyback. When she wrapped her arms around my neck, I appreciated the physical contact between us, and felt in my heart this was a positive step in the right direction.

She directed me where to walk by pointing with her finger and each time we passed Dan, he instinctively threatened to tickle her feet. Essie engaged well enough with Dan but her refusal to look at him directly was easy to read, Dan was not to come close of his own accord. After repeating this game, of getting close to Dan but never close enough for him to be able to tickle her feet, Essie instructed me to dump her on the armchair. This required me backing up and letting go of her, so she fell onto the armchair landing in a sitting position. I was happy that Essie was comfortable with our physical closeness, and no sooner had I dropped her, she was back up on her feet to play it again.

1 3 3

Essie got excited when I dropped her and I thought she may like the thrill of speed which reminded me of my son, who was just the same. I'm not sure if Essie had played this game before, or if she was just making it up in the moment, but she knew what the game was about. This was made clear when she said, "You're a dumpster truck collecting and I'm the rubbish getting dropped."

We then played a miming game, lying on the floor facing each other, with Dan laying behind me also facing Essie. She signaled for me to tickle Dan and I in return mimed 'Eye, Heart, You' before doing so. She was now involving Dan more, but this game didn't last long either.

Kay was sitting at her dining table in front of the laptop, when I noticed she was taking photographs of us while we were playing with Essie. Duncan had removed himself completely into their conservatory, along with their dog Albert. Essie wanted to play the piggyback dumpster game again. With both Kay and Dan looking on, I then decided to make some changes to the game. I crouched down for Essie to jump on my back from the armchair, I told her to hold on tight because I was changing the game. I spun around fast and fell onto the armchair with her, instead of letting her go. Telling her, "I don't pick up rubbish, I pick up special loads and once I do - I never, ever, let them go!"

I stood back up, with Essie still on my back and spun her around again. Only this time I realised I was out of practice because the dizziness came too quickly. I stopped spinning and we both fell back onto the armchair. I said, "Oh Essie I'm so dizzy, I nearly fell over." She found it all rather funny. Her laugh is amazing, it's infectious. After our out-burst of laughing Dan approached and again tried to tickle her feet, Essie didn't pull away this time and allowed him to tickle her foot.

Our first-time meeting Essie had flown by and all too soon our scheduled visit was over. On our journey back home, Dan said, "I wonder if Essie understands we were there to claim her as our own?"

It would be much later we'd come to understand that she was hoping we were going to rescue her.

Day 2: I woke before the alarm rang. I placed my hand on Dan's arm telling him it was time for us to get up. He opened his eyes and said, "I couldn't get to sleep last night, I was thinking about Essie."

He reminded me of a dream he had, many years ago. In his dream he had a daughter called Essie. But Dan has a younger sister who coincidentally is also named Essie and it made sense to us back then that the dream he had was about being a father figure to his little sister. Dan's sister is the same age as our son. They've grown up together and she is more like our daughter than his sister. But because of the journey we were now on, we both wondered if it could have been a precognitive dream.

It was Duncan and Kay's turn to bring Essie to us. I had been praying for them to be able to make Essie their priority.

Dan said, "They better put her first otherwise, I will have to put them straight." And I trusted he would, in the correct manner, if need be.

Essie came into our home and wanted to go straight into her bedroom, which she immediately claimed as her own. Our daughter walked into the bedroom, sat on the floor, and said, "Hello Essie I'm your sister," whilst holding out both her arms for a cuddle. Essie slowly walked over, taking a seat on her lap and accepted the cuddle. It was there in that moment, witnessing my daughter and our destiny's daughter's embrace, that I felt getting Essie had indeed been written in the stars. Essie was excited to check out the trampoline in the garden, our daughter held Essie's hand and took her out to explore.

Kay was brilliant, and I will give credit where it's due. If she felt awkward, nervous, or uncomfortable she didn't let it show. Duncan on the other hand was quite sheepish. We welcomed them to take a seat in our front room. Duncan seemed much smaller, sitting in our home, than he did when I had first met him. His posture was completely different sitting on our settee, his shoulders were rounded, and his head was slightly pulled in, it looked like he was cowering into himself; the way a turtle pulls their head back into its shell.

With our 13-year-old daughter doing a brilliant job of engaging with Essie, the time didn't fly by. To see our daughter lavish on Essie all her time and energy was truly amazing.

There were many awkward minutes of silence between Kay, Duncan, and me and without Dan's effort, I believe we'd have been sitting in total silence for most of the time. I felt relieved when it was time for them to go. I found it so hard to connect with the adults and although I had become accustomed to feeling awkward or out of place within official settings, I certainly did not appreciate this feeling inside my own home.

Day 3: We drove to Duncan and Kay's to pick Essie up; it had been scheduled for us to take her out and this would be our first time alone with her. Dan and I had pushed hard when having our input into the 'Introduction Plan' that our daughter should be present for our first-time taking Essie out. We were pleased we had gotten our way with this. After all, in just three days we were to become a family.

Kay opened the door, where we found Essie was ready and waiting for us to take her out. I reached out my hand and Essie took hold of it. Dan then told her she could help us plan the day. Her first choice was my pet hate, McDonalds. The queue was ridiculous, and it was rammed-packed. I hadn't stepped foot inside a McDonald's for a long time and seeing their state-of-the-art iPads I couldn't help thinking what a brilliant idea. They would work to help entice the kids to hag (beg) their parents to go back...again and again.

Outside there was a seating and play area with a bright red cube that had steps leading up to a tunnel slide. Essie was excited and asked if she could play. I walked around the apparatus to inspect it, one way in and the same way-out: excellent design. For a second, I shuddered at the memory my mind had recalled. I was supervising five children, on a school trip to a local farm. Taking them for a comfort break I was warned, by my colleague, that the toilet had

THE MYSTERY IN BEING A GYPSY

two entrances. My anxiety shot up like a rocket to the moon due to the risk of losing sight of a child because of its poor design!

It was lovely to see that even after all Essie had experienced from this crazy thing called life, she still possessed the natural gift to be sociable. She invited me to come into the cube with her and we played for a little while until Dan brought out our food. After eating, Dan told Essie it was time to go so we could have some more fun. As we were leaving, I noticed a school friend who I had not seen in many years. Nadine Hayward and I had lived near each other many years ago and went to the same secondary school in Dartford. Nadine asked, "What are you doing down here?"

I explained about adopting Essie and shared with Nadine, that I was feeling a little anxious as this was our first time out with Essie. And even though I hadn't seen Nadine for two decades, time had not changed my feelings about her. Nadine had always been a kind person and we had a good teenage friendship. Nadine spontaneously wrapped her arms around me, embracing me in a tight hug. It was just what I needed. In a chance meeting, I had bumped into an old friend, who'd given me a physical hug of encouragement which served to boost my confidence.

Essie's next choice was to go to the park, I wondered if she wanted to put Dan's strength to the test, we'd wrote in the letter we had sent to her that Dan was strong and could push the swings high. And that's exactly what she did she tested his strength. Essie was squealing excitedly to be pushed higher and higher. Sitting in the park watching my husband making sure Essie was having fun, just as he had done so many times before with our children when they were younger, completely melted my heart. I didn't know it was possible to fall in love with the same person all over again.

When Essie got bored with the park, Dan reminded me that her bedroom still needed a light. I asked Essie, "Would you like to go shopping for a light?" And surprisingly, she was excited to do so. We drove to the nearest B&Q (a home improvement retail store) and Essie chose a sparkly chandelier. Dan told her that he would be fitting her light just as soon as we got home. His reward was her smile.

Our scheduled time out with Essie was nearing its end and Dan then drove us all back to Kay and Duncan's. All three of us took part in Essie's bedtime routine and after reading her a story and kissing her forehead, wishing her a goodnight, it was time for us to leave.

Day 4: We arrived a few minutes early, Kay let us in and called upstairs to Essie telling her we were here to pick her up. We were invited in to take a seat where Kay then explained to us, "Essie may need permission, in the mornings, to come out of her bedroom." Kay continued, "We have the same rule for our daughter Angelia because we aren't really morning people. We like to get up in the morning and have 'our' time with a cuppa. We find out what's on the news, come around to ourselves for a bit and then call for Essie to come down and join us for breakfast."

I didn't know how to respond to this information, so I didn't. I momentarily glazed over because I have never known such parenting skills. I was conscious that I was giving Kay a blank stare and she looked slightly uncomfortable. I'll confess this was perfectly okay with me because God above knows I was trying so hard not to give a judgmental response. I just do not relate to this 'me' time as a parent.

Essie came crashing down the stairs, just at the perfect moment, and Dan told her we were off bowling. When we walked out of their home, Dan and I held each other's gaze just for a moment and we both knew we were thinking the same thing: let's show Essie some fun.

The bowling alley was very busy, so we played in the arcade, killing some time until it was our turn to bowl. Our daughter went straight into her 'big sister' roll playing table air hocky with Essie. Predictably Essie won and the delight on her face radiated like the sun. We noticed very quickly Essie's competitive nature, is one that doesn't like to lose. After bowling, we ate out in a restaurant, and it was then I first wondered if Essie has a short attention span. She stood up on the seats, climbed under the table, climbed back up on the seat then laid down on them, all before we'd ordered. I wasn't sure if she was behaving like a little busy bee because she was

THE MYSTERY IN BEING A GYPSY

excited, however, it was already clear to us that Essie is an easily excitable child.

Dan asked her, "When we have finished eating would you like to go to the park again?"

Essie didn't waste a second in telling us, "I'd love to go to Tiny Town, I've never been."

We weren't sure how true this information was, after discovering Tiny Town was a soft play area, close to where Duncan and Kay lived, and it was just a few pounds entry. I couldn't imagine Essie had not been before during her year at Duncan and Kay's but we took her anyway. Our daughter was again brilliant with Essie, following her around, whilst she was busy exploring Tiny Town. We returned Essie home on time, and as soon as Kay opened the door Essie squealed, "I've been to Tiny Town!"

Kay told us, "Essie has been wanting go there for quite a while, but it was just one of those things we haven't managed to get around to doing."

She asked me, "Was it good?"

And I told her, "Essie loved it."

We then went upstairs to do the bedtime routine and to my delight, Essie asked, "Can my sister read me a story?"

Day 5: It was Kay and Duncan's turn to drop Essie at ours. When they arrived, Essie was desperately excited to play on the trampoline. Her first lesson was, we don't go on the trampoline if it's wet, and the simple reasoning given to her was she could fall and hurt herself. Essie both understood and accepted this.

With the prep groups and training days at the forefront of my mind (regarding some behaviours we may experience) it was also important to prepare the other little girls who live on our site. I explained to our neighbour's daughters that there would be times when Essie would need me, and I may have to give her all my attention. It was important for me to explain this to our neighbours little girls, because they were used to coming into Aunty Genty's anytime they liked. I had to teach these little girls aged: ten, seven, and two of them who were three years old, that Essie was coming to our home to live forever, and it would be very strange for her; so, there will be times I'd have to say no to them coming in.

We told Essie about the girls who live on our site who'd been looking forward to meeting her. I asked, "Would you like to meet them, Essie? I can invite them into play." Essie spent no time thinking about it and replied, "Yes."

The girls came in and I introduced them to each other. My neigbours' daughters were brilliant! They lavished Essie with compliments, telling her, "We have been so looking forward to meeting you." They each complimented Essie, telling her that she was pretty, and that they like her clothes. Essie was a little shy at first, but she soon joined in with the girls who were playing with the toys in our home.

We got to see the first signs of Essie's understandable need to be in control; a warning given to us at the prep groups. One of the girls handed Essie a Barbie doll to play with, Essie took the doll and then threw it on the floor. She was instantly upset and stormed off into her room slamming the door behind her. I asked the girls to go outside to play and told them they could come back later after Essie had been picked up; explaining to them that everything is strange and new for Essie and that she just needs time to get used to us all.

I walked into the bedroom and sat on the floor, positioning myself so that Essie needed to look down at me, I didn't want to stand over her and be in a higher position because I didn't want to seem threatening (my years working at Riverview Primary school had gifted me this skill that had now become an instinct).

I asked Essie, "Would you like a cuddle because you're a little upset?" Essie forcefully shook her head, "No!" So, I sat in silence with her until she was ready to communicate first.

When she did, she told me, "People aren't allowed to touch your stuff without asking permission". I asked her why she felt the girls shouldn't play with the toys without her permission and she abruptly replied, "It's a rule."

I explained that everyone has different rules. I could see she was listening so I said, "We will need to learn new rules together, and you can help teach me the rules that you know."

I gave her assurance that differences aren't a bad thing, and in fact, it can be a good thing to learn different rules explaining that the other girls already knew one of the rules in our home; we share the toys.

Essie had given me full eye contact so I said, "I think you're going to learn quickly I can see you're an intelligent little girl". These words brought the smile.

We spent the rest of our day watching Disney, colouring, and involving Essie in food prep for our lunch. When Kay and Duncan arrived to collect her, waving her off, I felt overwhelmed relating to this little girl's feelings. Everything must be so confusing for her.

The sixth and final day: I woke feeling confident that the day could go well, even against the odds of expected tears and tantrums. Dan and I felt confident enough to coach Essie into leaving the home she had lived in for the last year, without her feeling that her world was once again about to fall apart.

I wrote a text to Kay on our drive down: "Good morning, I have been worrying a little, but we think, time to go all out for major distraction. I'm sure we can hype Essie up into wanting to go to her new home. There are bound to be tears but I'm also confident, with us working together, of her smiles. Our plan is to take her for breakfast then off to Tiny Town. Hopefully, Tiny Town will help burn up some of the energy from all the very large emotions she will no doubt be feeling. Would you help build the hype by asking Essie, I wonder if you will be going back to Tiny Town today?"

Kay replied to the text: "It will be fine don't worry; I will get her excited for Tiny Town, and we will pack the last of her bits into the car when you arrive."

I wondered how Kay would be feeling. Was she emotionally struggling? I could only imagine how getting attached to a child, after loving and caring for them for a year, would be easy to do. What Kay was about to face this morning was the single concern which had led me to hold reservations about fostering; the attachment formed, then 'coping emotionally' with the separation.

I also wondered how many of Essie's belongings were left to be packed as we had already taken some of her things. It looked like she had quite a lot, but surprisingly, when organising and packing it away into our home, we discovered she was in desperate need of so much. She came with an outgrown wardrobe of clothes that had all been very well worn.

I texted Kay again, letting her know we were a couple of minutes away. Pulling into their street we could see Duncan, Kay and Essie were stood outside waiting for us. Kay and Duncan apathetically handed over the last of Essie's belongings, along with a new bike they had brought her. They said goodbye to Essie, and Kay kissed her on the cheek whilst reminding her about the importance of brushing her teeth. Parting cuddles were given, and we then set off to start our lives together.

After a week, Margaret (Essie's social worker) visited us. She shared with me, "What a delight it was to see that Essie was already more relaxed and able to communicate with her better than she had previously known her to be able to do."

Witnessing Essie's calmer and engaging demeanour had confirmed for Margaret that she had made the right commitment, to ensure Essie was placed with us.

Margaret said, "Essie's situation has taught me to be more assertive as a social worker and I feel empowered in my own ability to make confident decisions and assert them in the child's best interest."

When Margaret was up against her superiors (who had never met Essie) and they had different ideas about the decisions that should be made for her future, Margaret told me, "Should I find myself in such a position again I would stand my ground, managing to be much more confident."

We were standing in the kitchen, and I was making our second round of coffee, I had given Essie TV time, which we learned within two days of having Essie, that she becomes so transfixed when watching the TV, she doesn't hear or notice anything else going on around her.

THE MYSTERY IN BEING A GYPSY

Margaret confessed, "I have also gained personal growth through the opportunities that Essie's case has presented, and I have found the ability to overcome my own prejudice and fears that I once held towards your community."

I was delighted to hear this and without thinking about it, I gave Margaret a tight cuddle, which she embraced.

Before it was time for Margaret to leave, I mentioned that Kay had been taking photos of us when we were at her house on the first day of introductions. I asked, what the photos are used for, and Margaret wasn't impressed to hear we'd not been asked permission for the photos to be taken.

Margaret said, "Taking photos is often done, if agreed to by all involved, but certainly not to just take them."

I replied, "It doesn't matter, and actually if we could have copies of the photos that would be lovely."

The scheduled 'goodbye' meeting at our home for Duncan, Kay and their daughter was booked for the 30th of October. Margaret called us, the day before informing me that, when she asked Kay about the photos she replied, "I was simply capturing a special moment, and I will get copies made for them."

I was pleased to hear this and was looking forward to receiving the photos. I imagined that tomorrow would be difficult for them as a family. Saying goodbye to a child they have cared for would surely be very emotionally taxing. Dan had taken Essie to the shop to get them a little gift from her. When they returned, Essie excitedly showed me what she had chosen for them, a bottle of wine with some chocolates for Kay and Duncan, and a necklace for Angelia. Essie was so pleased with her little gifts, and she couldn't wait to give them out.

As soon as they'd arrived at ours Essie dragged Angelia by her hand into her bedroom, to show off her light. She then excitedly ran to get the gifts she had chosen for them, but there was little gratitude shown. In fact, Dan and I had made more fuss (giving praise and thanks) over receiving a cupcake from Essie than they made about receiving their gifts from her. The scheduled goodbye visit was all quite apathetic, and they made their excuses to leave,

1 4 3

not even having managed to spend the full allocated time at ours that had been arranged. To be honest I couldn't wait for them to get out of our home, just as much as they were desperate to leave it.

There were no tears, no emotions displayed and no real affection in the parting cuddles with Essie either. After we waved them off and I had closed the door, I turned to Essie to check she was alright. I wasn't sure how she would be feeling this child had known more goodbyes than most adults. Essie's nose was scrunched up and she was wearing a frown, this was not the expression of sadness that I had anticipated in fact she looked annoyed!

I asked her, "What's wrong Essie?" And she replied, "They didn't look very pleased with their gifts, did they?"

I shot Dan a look, because Essie had caught me off guard showing that she felt the same as I did. Her big sister was quick to respond and told Essie, "Don't worry about them being ungrateful."

Essie picked up her brown boots, that were in our hallway, swung open the front door and threw the boots out saying, "Goodbye, never seeing youse again!"

We discovered her brown boots were not her choice when I jokingly said, "Oh Essie why are you taking it out on the boots, they haven't done anything wrong".

Essie recalled the day when the boots were bought, how she had been told off quite a lot for her behaviour because she didn't want practical boots, it was clear to me Essies wasn't able to understand that the 'practical' boots were indeed needed over the 'pretty' boots she preferred. So, the boots bore the brunt of her feelings.

I was asked by Margaret to write an email about Duncan and Kay about how smoothly the introductions schedule went. I was honest with Margaret that when I cannot say something nice, "It's better that I say nothing at all."

I was told the letter would be added to Kay and Duncan's fostering files, and that it was a common practice for adopters to share what they felt the fosterers did well. I refused. My honesty, which at times can be too harsh for most, would not allow me to

THE MYSTERY IN BEING A GYPSY

cherry-pick. Being seen as polite and PC does not trump the truth for me.

The photos that Kay had taken of 'our' very special first day with Essie: we never did receive copies. I can't help assuming, if I had written a nice email about them, we'd have those special family photos today.

We knew some of Essie's past and we could, for the most part, piece together the puzzle of what her life has been like from what's written in her files. There were certainly many professionals who were responsible for her wellbeing. Yet nothing had been picked up about her behaviours and triggers. Nothing noted, no warnings, or advice. Yet it's easy to see that bubbling under the surface of Essie there's a real resentment that's built up, that's just sitting there, and it won't take much for it to spill over.

Kay and Duncan's warning given at our first meeting about the 'snipey-girl' and how during her year with them she has had several major outbursts of violent and out-of-control bedroom tantrums, we have never seen, and I still cannot understand how it was never considered important to arrange professional help for her.

Eventually we arranged a meeting with Essie's aunt-L, that took place a year after having Essie in our family. With aunt-L's knowledge we were able to then place the missing pieces of Essie's life into the puzzle, to see the full picture.

As I am writing this now, I can't believe how seven years have flown past. This little survivor has been angry at times, but it's nothing a tight cuddle couldn't help her out of. She believed her capabilities were way beyond her years, and that she didn't need a responsible adult to take care of her. In her heart and mind, she believed she could take care of herself and call all the shots. And there was some truth to this because there were times in her life when she did indeed need to take care of herself. Essie had learned from a very young age how to be an adult, and it's natural for her to live in survival mode. Something we are still working through with her to this day. We also got a diagnosis that helped open the door for Essie to receive play therapy.

Essie has adapted to her new home very well. We have never experienced 'any' animated outbursts when Essie spots trailers (caravans). Essie had been considered lucky by Social Services to have been placed for a year with foster carers who met her needs. She had certainly learned boundaries from her stay there, boundaries that saw Essie asking permission to leave her bedroom, or the food table, or to snack, to watch TV, or to get a drink, and it took several months for Essie to understand she wouldn't be in trouble for leaving her bedroom in the morning once she had woken up.

Essie was desperately in need of love and so ready for full inclusion in a family home. No matter how a child's basic needs are met, living in six different homes, as Essie had - means she was bound to have been affected, and time has revealed it all. I could easily write a book about Essie's life and the seven years we have had of loving her. But I'm not going to share any more of her story. One day when she is older, and if she chooses to share it all, that will be her right to do so.

After the adoption, I continued to attend all the meetings I could, whilst Essie was in school. I was invited by Friends, Family and Travellers (FFT), who are a national charity, to speak in The Palace of Westminster, in a parliament event, about our experience with Social Services during our adoption process. Even though I am not comfortable with having all eyes on me publicly speaking, I accepted because I felt passionate that our 'Gypsy prejudice struggle' needs to be shared to help highlight what can be done to make positive changes. It was quite an experience to be a speaker as opposed to being an attendee.

Around the same time, Margaret had called to ask for my permission to share my contact details with a couple (who had recently adopted a little boy) because they wanted the opportunity to learn about his culture and ethnic heritage. So much good has come out of all this; Dan and I were invited to attend one of the adoption courses, but this time as adopters, to share our experience. We were ecstatic when we learned that Kent Social Services had taken Essie's case to teach about.

THE MYSTERY IN BEING A GYPSY

When our other two children were newborns. Dan and I would get lost in time just looking at our children's very existence. We'd spend hours taking in every detail of their being. It's about much more than the physical looks that are being absorbed and stored into the memory bank, it's so much deeper, it's the spiritual connection that binds together hearts and souls. It's the instant protection felt, like the lioness who would kill or die to protect her cubs. It's the alpha male, or the wolf father protecting his den at all costs. For the third time, with our third child, our souls have connected, our one and only 'destiny' daughter has allowed us to love her.

14

PUBLIC SPEAKING

With the introduction for the duty, placed on local authority for site provisions whereby local authority were originally allowed to provide the minimum amount of plots needed, and following the demise of traditional stopping places alongside the Planning Policy definition change: in August 2015, when the Government actually got away with changing the definition of 'Gypsies' (to no longer include those who had ceased travelling for any reason), which also restricted Gypsies from providing plots for themselves, it was inevitable a national site shortage would follow.

On the 4th of November 2014, a report by the Equality and Human Rights Commission suggested that one square mile is all that is needed to end the shortage. I recommend another Travellers' Times article 'One square mile' 4th of November 2014, www.travellerstimes.co.uk.

My friend Hilda Brazil and my cousin Anne Wilson MBE were both long-standing committee members of the Surrey, Gypsy, Traveller, Communities Forum (SGTCF). Hilda was the Co-Chair and Anne was the secretary. They had both dedicated years of their lives to help highlight the accommodation shortages and political resolutions. Sadly, Anne passed away without seeing a day that brings an end to this madness, and Hilda has since retired.

They had both voluntarily given so much of their own time collaborating with local authorities and the police to help resolve the cat and mouse game that's being played. One where nomadic Travellers pull on land, get evicted, pull-on land somewhere else, only to be evicted again. They were also both robust advocates for maintenance of the existing Gypsy sites, and site provisions for the offspring of the permanently living residents belonging to Surrey.

Anne called to tell me a meeting had been arranged, at the Surrey Police Headquarters to discuss unauthorised encampments with

Councillor (Cllr) David Munro, and how it was also an opportunity to extend an invite for Cllr Munro to attend the upcoming SGTCF Conference. Anne explained that both she and Hilda had other work commitments, on the date which was suitable for Cllr Munro and neither of them could attend. So, Anne had asked if I could go on their behalf.

David Munro had been a local Councillor for twenty-six years; he was also the Surrey Police and Crime Commissioner. Anne explained all that was needing to be discussed at this meeting, would be taken care of by John and Mark (two other SGTCF committee members) and I would stand in as SGTCF ethnic community representative. The meeting took place in Cllr Munro's office, John and Mark did all the talking and highlighted the simple solution to unauthorised encampments: a transit site or a negotiated stopping area.

I didn't speak until Cllr Munro said, "There's a two-way problem with unauthorised encampments first, is the hostility from the local permanent residents and then there's the anti-social behaviour of the Travellers."

I added, "There is a third, 'media' they have the power and ability to coach the masses to form views by their use of persuasive writing."

I then shared that the biased and unbalanced reporting, of only the anti-social behaviours and no reporting on the solution for unauthorised encampments has helped to fuel the hostility. I informed Cllr Munro that I have never in my life lived nomadically. I did so to highlight the fact that over 99% of English Romany-Gypsies are permanently living residents of Surrey, and that Romanies have ancestral heritage in Surrey spanning centuries, and that my ethnic community are in housing, on yards, or on private or council sites and that to own the view that all termed Travellers have no fixed abode, set up unauthorised camps and behave anti-socially, is completely inaccurate.

The truth is, it's a minority of 'all' nomadic people who behave environmentally disrespectfully when leaving their rubbish behind. No different than those of us who are from settled communities. We also have our fair share of those who behave anti-socially. And let's make no pretence, there are plenty who litter. The following Traveller Times' article, about the rubbish left behind after festivals, I used to evidence that littering is a societal problem and not specific to ethnicity, creed or colour:

Founder of The Romany-Gypsy Guild, Genty Lee, explains the reason and hope behind the 'Gypsies and Travellers against rubbish campaign'.

In August 2018, my husband and I attended the Reading Festival aftermath. We went to collect one-man tents and sleeping bags for our local homeless group 'The Big Warm Up' who are an amazing local group who voluntary help feed, clothe, and provide sleeping bags for people living on the streets. The main organiser Anthony Burdett is a family friend and we wanted to help support the great work he and the others, from 'our' Gorger community do. Anthony is truly an inspirational young man, and the world is in desperate need of a few more with his calibre.

We arrived to collect the tents and I was immediately struck by the amount of waste. There was a vast sea of camping tents most of which were bought new for the festival. It made me understand what's meant by throw-away society. Next to hit, was the mess!

Above is a screenshot, from a video I made, of the 'rubbish bombsite' left behind after the Reading festival.

We had to literally watch every step, as the field had been used as a toilet and the amount of rubbish: I've personally never seen anything like it! The organisers had provided toilets and bins, it was infuriating to see the bins empty, and rubbish strewn all over the fields, and human excrement everywhere. Standing still looking around, for as far as the eye could see, was rubbish, tents, camping chairs, and sleeping bags (which had all been left behind). It struck a raw nerve with me in that moment, because of how society in general, tries to make me feel responsible for the mess some nomadic Travellers leave behind (after an unauthorised encampment). I wondered, who's made to feel bad or judged for this festival bombsite?

It also occurred to me that this aftermath of waste, filth and rubbish wasn't written about in any of the local or national newspapers, slandering the behaviour has 'typical' of the festival community. Yet every week there's a story on an unauthorised encampment and the rubbish left behind. Yet, the same news platforms never report about the local authorities not fulfilling their duty of site provision. Instead, the report is centred around the rubbish left behind. When anti-social behaviour and crimes are committed by those termed Travellers the crime gets portrayed 'incorrectly' as being linked to ethnicity or culture! Yet when a crime is committed by those of privilege (such as those who can afford to spend hundreds of pounds on camping equipment, to use once, and then leave it all behind for someone else to clear up), this behaviour 'oddly' isn't seen as anti-social.

I shared the video footage of the filth left by the Gorger people who attended the festival, in our Romany-Gypsy Guild Facebook group. We then decided to start our own campaign for nomadic Travellers and Born-again Christians (who attend conventions and missions) to either video or take photos of the areas they've stopped on showing how they left the area to prove Gypsies and Travellers do not 'typically' litter and fly-tip. This idea was inspired by the Muslims who took part in the 'Not in My Name Campaign' against terrorists.

We put together the aerial photos taken before and after the Light and Life Gypsy convention, and the before and after aerial photos of the Glastonbury festival. We did this as a comparison to try and counter the negative mainstream media reports on unauthorised encampments that stereotype 'collectively' all people who are termed 'Travellers'.

THE MYSTERY IN BEING A GYPSY

***The top two images (below) are of the Gypsy Light and
Life mission, 'Before and After' - left immaculate!***

***The bottom two images (above) are of the Glastonbury
festival, 'Before and After' - left as a rubbish bomb site!***

The Travellers' Times article read: We as a people group are among the most hygienically clean of all peoples and it's important that we show ourselves to be. The Guild hopes to see this campaign take off to help prove that the 'majority' of Travellers leave places spotless, and at times better than they were found! The battle has begun. Let's stand together in the 'Gypsy and Travellers against rubbish campaign' and show ourselves for who we really are! (Travellers' Times, www.travellerstimes.org.uk, 23rd of May 2019).

Anti-social behaviours regardless of being committed by people belonging to any of the ethnic minorities or the people who belong to the ethnic majority, should never be viewed as 'collective behaviour of all'. To hold all people groups termed Travellers accountable and generalise that this is typical behaviour of all, is completely wrong and there's a word for doing this - the word is 'bias'. The media platforms, who report unbalanced views of Gypsies and Travellers need to take responsibility, for attitudes - they help to create - which blame the culture or ethnicity as a collective, opposed to the individuals themselves.

Cllr Munro didn't agree that we could place the blame at the feet of the media, but he didn't disagree either. When the media report on any ethnic minority group it is done so by continuously highlighting the bad, (a common reporting strategy against our Black brothers and sisters also). The general populous are also guilty of forming negative views, blaming the entire group by default of ethnicity, skin colour, creed, or culture. Yet, the reality is, there's isn't a culture, skin colour, creed or ethnicity who are exempt from having their own fair share of people who behave anti-socially or criminally.

John and Mark were pleased with the outcome of the meeting. Cllr Munro had accepted the invite to our upcoming conference. He also agreed that the resolve for Surrey's unauthorised encampments was indeed as simple as providing a single transit site or having an available area, for negotiated stopping, in Surrey. When he agreed with this practical solution, it was considered by both Mark and John that the SGTCF had a good advocate in Cllr Munro. One who carried some real weight of power and influence because of the position he held.

I was the first to speak at the conference. I was feeling confident and pleased to be sharing the testimonies that I had collected. Even though I dislike public speaking I wasn't feeling nervous as I felt prepared. All that I intended to say I had printed on a hard copy ready to be read out. I had spent quite a bit of time, practicing reading at home, using my own family as my audience. I was taking my position in this new world of conferences very seriously.

THE MYSTERY IN BEING A GYPSY

Everyone who had received an invitation showed up, which provided a good number of attendees. I was asked by Mark if I would take part in a short interview with Surrey live after our conference had finished. He informed me Cllr Munro had asked his permission to invite Surrey Live, who are a media platform, for them to be given the opportunity to interview members of the Traveller communities but having no trust in the media whatsoever I declined.

Louisa, Anne, Hilda, and I took our seats on the panel. I had the advice of Russel in my mind who had told me to have a glass of water ready in case my mouth went dry because it was okay to stop for a drink. I sat down and did one last check to make sure my papers were in order, knowing before I did that they were.

Hilda began the conference by welcoming everyone and said, "We are going to get started quickly and I am handing over to our first speaker."

My inner champion voice encouraged, "You've got this!" And I began to read:

My name is Genty Lee, I am the Lead in Education for the Surrey Gypsy Traveller Community Forum. In our Guild Facebook group, which has over five thousand members, we asked about the impact the lack of site provision is having. We received an overwhelming response and 100% of the replies received reported the impact is a negative one. The anti-Gypsy laws, Acts, and legislation that have been passed, mainly under the Tory government, have caused this problem of unauthorised stopping. And yet, there's still been no action taken to provide the solution.

What is apparent is the deep-rooted generational mistrust of those in authority, and in those who hold positions of power because such people have seldom brought our ethnic group anything constructive. This desperate need for local authorities to adhere to the Caravan Sites Act section 24, 'to compensate with sites' is long overdue. The constant draconian measures targeted at ethnic Romany-Gypsies and other Travellers have caused the infiltrations that we now see taking place against all nomadic people. I will now read some firsthand testimonies:

Kathleen reported: When local authorities stopped building sites, we were encouraged to buy our own land to provide for ourselves. We were promised to be granted planning permission. But this certainly wasn't the case for many. After 14 years and two appeals, finally we were granted permission to live on our own land. It's been so stressful. Buying green belt sounded like a solution, but it was only for those who could afford to take the chance of buying land and only for those who had the will to fight the planning laws to overturn the sanction of green belt. The conditions we had to follow made us feel like aliens because of the discrimination we faced. For example, we were ordered to plant hedging to hide us from view, we were also told to paint our home green, to be less visible. For generations, all we have ever known is discrimination, promises, and lies. Eric Pickles springs to mind.

I will share some information about Eric Pickles, that will help explain why Kathleen mentioned him, at the end of these preceding replies. Because those who attended the conference would have already been very well aware of Mister. Eric Pickles antics.

Sharon shared: Residents on a council site who rent a plot, live in harsh conditions because the council sites provided, most of them were on built on waste ground, that wasn't suitable for anything else, and many sites have been placed in areas that are secluded, near dangers or susceptible to flooding. The fact that all nomadic people have no authorised places to stop on, cause more discrimination for us all. All that ever makes the news is stories about illegal encampments and the rubbish left behind. Readers do not understand such encampments are NOT illegal, they are unauthorised. Not many know about the laws that have been passed, that have caused all of the problems we see now. And it's strange that the media don't make headline stories about the rubbish left behind by beachgoers or cover stories about the mess

THE MYSTERY IN BEING A GYPSY

left behind by football supporters or in towns after the clubbing weekenders. If a person termed a Traveller commits a crime or behaves anti-socially it's reported in the media that alludes [to a presumption] this is typical of the ethnicity or culture. Yet, when a Gorger from the ethnic majority commits a crime, they are seen as an individual. There is no fairness for Romany-Gypsies, not equal opportunities in education or accommodation. There never has been, I hope there will be for the sake of my children, and the future generations yet to come.

Kevin reported: As a recently retired person, working in a Housing department in Surrey, with the grand title of Gypsy Liaison Officer, I saw first-hand what impact the lack of site provision had. The two sites I managed were built in the late 1970s, but no further pitches have been provided since that time, so over 40 years on, nothing has been done for the offspring of those original residents. All this does is increase the pressure on the two sites with 'doubling up' on many pitches. I was always sympathetic to family members who had nowhere to go and was prepared to allow doubling up so long as it didn't compromise fire safety. But I shouldn't have been put in this position in the first place. The biggest issue in a County like Surrey, apart from hostility from the Gorger residents, is land value. If a house can be built, they will be because developers make a fortune from that land. Therefore, site provision is always bottom of the pile. Also, in the area where I worked, 70% of the land is Green Belt. The sanctity of the Green Belt needs to be loosened. There needs to be one rule for all in Planning laws. Billionaire business chains seem skilled at getting Green Belt sanctions overturned. And finally, the 2015 planning definition change of who is a 'Gypsy' has allowed local authorities to use this as an excuse to drastically reduce the number of pitches required in their area.

Racheal shared: I live on a council site. I have three children in school, I do worry about their future. It's not possible for me to travel and I have never lived nomadically. Since the planning definition has been changed regarding Gypsy status, I'm very worried that before long I will be forced to travel for three months of the year to meet the planning criteria of Gypsy to be able to continue renting my plot. I already worry as a mother, knowing that it doesn't matter if my children are very successful in education, they will not get the same chance unless we hide their ethnicity, and this is hard to do, living on a site because our ethnicity is automatically presumed. There are Gorger people, who have married in, who also live on sites. There are also Gorger people who live nomadically (new age travellers). Nomadism is a chosen lifestyle for some, for others its cultural or for business purposes. Romany-Gypsies are an ethnic group who have faced years of racism. The government has placed anyone who either has a past culture of living nomadically, or who still live partially or completely nomadically, to all now be termed Travellers, packaged into one box. Compensation [of site provision] was not sufficiently adhered to, and with muddying the water by encompassing us all as Travellers, and with the adoption of the acronym 'GRT' I don't believe it ever will be.

Tina reported: There shouldn't be homelessness for any person. We all pay enough in tax. As for the argument that there's not enough land to build on, then I have a simple solution. I got the idea from the Tory government, cap the size of individual land ownership. Some houses occupied in Surrey, (which I have seen myself), are a wasteful and unnecessary use of acres of land. How many people: Gorgers, Gypsies and Travellers alike could be homed if more site-like spaces were available? Site provisions should have always been provided, we are not newcomers, our ancestors have been here for many centuries. We are just now more visible, we haven't just arrived one, two or three generations ago (we haven't invaded England, we are English), we have simply stopped hiding away for protection in the woods.

Shannon shared: If there's a strain on the police to deal with unauthorised encampments, then I say, "You reap what you sow." Any police officer who doesn't know the history of our persecution, the prejudice, racism, and the unfair treatment we have been subjected to shouldn't deal with unauthorised encampments. The last of my family to live nomadically was in the 70s when police

THE MYSTERY IN BEING A GYPSY

brutality was subjected on people who had nowhere to pull [stop], due to government legislation. This treatment has left its mark on us. I have no trust in the police. Most English Romany-Gypsies I know have worked long and hard. Ask any farmer who has kept the farming industry flowing in this country for the last century. Stop painting us as the dossers of society.

Emma shared: Honest hard-working people we are, and have been raised to be, we pay our way and always have. It's just no one cares to see this. Most police I've met talk to us like we are children, and that they are above us. A lot needs to be done, but it's not us that need to change anymore to fit into society. We need equality. We are always judged as a collective, based on the worst criminals who have the same ethnic origin. I want to ask, "Are all in the police in the force good? Are all other ethnicities free of criminals and those who behave anti-socially? Are all politicians and those who hold positions of authority honest and never committed a crime? No, they're not! There's good and bad in all. My grandparents weren't viewed as bad, non-taxpaying, anti-social litterers - when they fought in both world wars for OUR country. We need to be allowed to have our own voices and see an end to the stereotypes that many police and local authority and the government believe us to be like. If the police and authorities can't help untangling the web they have woven and agree to the solution of site provision then, Just Leave Us Alone.

I thanked everyone for listening and followed on with saying, "I hope that after today, we will have some attendees present, who stand in influential work positions, who are willing to help ensure the long-overdue recommendations for site provision are adhered to. Let's advocate for the simple solution of site provisions."

During question time, after our speakers had presented, a man from the audience raised his hand to speak. He began by making a statement: I have no prejudice toward Travellers. I lived near some Travellers whilst growing up and I attended a school where Travellers were present. He continued, "They are lovely people, but my question is why do they disrespect the land, they illegally occupy - by littering it with rubbish - why can't they just respect the local people?"

I gave a nod to Michelle Gavin, (a guest speaker) and she immediately shot him down, with her response. She asked him, "Why do you believe that was an appropriate question to ask when there isn't a single person, here today present, who lives nomadically?" Michelle didn't pause to allow the man a reply and she further added,

"Least of all are there any who are present today who are guilty of fly-tipping or littering. Too many people hold the view, that all Travellers should stand accountable by ethnic origin or culture, for the wrongs another has done. Yet, these same people do not feel responsible for the wrongdoing of those belonging to their own ethnicity. Only a person themselves can be held accountable, it's not fair that anyone else sharing the ethnicity or the culture should be questioned as though they are guilty."

Needless to say, no such further questions in the same tone, followed.

After the conference, I was speaking with a couple of local Surrey police officers. I felt irritated by Cllr Munro's use of the word 'incursion' in relation to unauthorised encampments, when he spoke as our guest speaker, ('incursion' is the one word that really grates my nerves because it means to invade and attack, a hostile entrance into enemy territory; it's war terminology). A man and woman who I had never seen before walked over to us, whilst I was in mid flow of expressing my feelings.

I would have much preferred to have spoken directly to Cllr Munro. However, he was busy speaking with the Surrey Live reporters, and I didn't get the opportunity to do so.

I continued with what I was saying, "I can forgive ignorance because that to me is the innocence of not knowing any better, but I don't feel as though Cllr Munro lacks in education."

I noticed that the two officer's demeanors had changed, and the man who had walked over, who had clearly heard what I was saying, in the face of the silence of the officers said, "We can all be guilty of being ignorant and it doesn't matter what type of education a person's received we can still be ignorant."

I could do no other but to agree that this can be true. The woman who had also come over congratulated me for sharing the testimonies. She said, "It's important to have first-hand accounts."

The man then introduced himself as Chris Raymer, not that his name meant anything to me at the time, but later I understood the demeanor change of the officers was because Chris Raymer is their higher-ranking Detective Superintendent (Surrey Police Force). The woman introduced herself as Florentina, I then learned she was a Romany-Gypsy who had moved from her home country, in Romania, and became a first response officer for 999 calls for Surrey police. They both expressed an interest in becoming members of the SGTCF, so I proudly pointed them in the direction of 'my cousin' Anne Wilson MBE, the secretary.

This conference was held back in 2017, but seven years on Surrey still doesn't have a transit site or an area available for negotiated stopping. There has been very little effort made for additional permanent sites. There have been some individual plots provided by adding a few here and there onto already existing sites, but not much of a real effort has been made to increase provision. However, it seems a common exercise to conduct and repeat the site assessment needs.

I honestly cannot, no matter how hard I try, understand why so many people have the mindset that the ethnicity is to blame for the wrongdoings or bad behaviours of people as individuals.

Having a mindset that believes all the innocent should be held accountable and viewed as 'collective wrongdoers' is completely unfathomable to me. I have often found myself defending and challenging the openly negative stereotypes that also generalise and discriminate by those who are racist against Black, Caribbean, Asian and Indian people because to many of the majority group (white British) own the mind set of 'collective blaming' – except when it's a white British criminal!

A mindset that paints all members of an ethnicity with the same dirty brush, is a mindset that has been taught a dangerously false ideology. I am very grateful to know better. It's our family's moral code of conduct, passed down through the generations, which allows me the 'knowing' that there's good and bad in all.

15

MEDIA INFLUENCE & POWER

The reason Eric Pickles was known to the conference attendees was because he had been found guilty of discriminating against Romany-Gypsies on the 21st of January 2015. The High Court judge said, "Both human rights and equality laws were breached by Pickles and his department by 'calling in' cases which would normally be considered by his planning inspectors where decisions should be taken on the merits of an application, and not the characteristics of the applicant."

Shortly after 'someone', 'somewhere' didn't think it would be inappropriate or insulting to offer Pickles the position of the 'Holocaust Envoy Role'. A position that he accepted! The Special Envoy for Post-Holocaust Issues' key objective is to ensure that the UK continues to play a prominent role in international discussions on all Holocaust-related matters, especially those relating to education and the opening of archives that continue to respond to the concerns of Holocaust victims and their families.

Uncle Joe (Joseph Jones) was infuriated that Pickles had been offered and had accepted the Holocaust position, not long after he was found guilty in a court of law for discrimination against members of our ethnic group. Uncle Joe's frustrations were shared in the Travellers' Times – which helped to get the word out to those, like me, who had no idea how those in positions of power don't mind adding insult to injury. The following Travellers' Times article, in my opinion, should have been published by mainstream media but they show little interest in giving members from our legitimate ethnic group a voice.

Joseph G Jones slams Eric Pickles' Holocaust Envoy role – because he discriminated against Gypsies. Sir Eric Pickles' role as the UK's Holocaust Envoy has been questioned by a veteran

Romany Gypsy campaigner because the former Government Minister was previously found to have discriminated against Romany Gypsies in court.

Joseph G Jones, from the Gypsy Council, spoke out in a post on the Gypsy Council Thames Valley Facebook page on April 8th International Roma Day, and said that Pickles' past history of discrimination against Gypsies made him unfit for the role.

"I saw some time ago that Eric Pickles the former Sec State - infamous for discriminating against Romani Gypsies - was appointed Special Envoy for Post-Holocaust issues in September 2015," said Joseph Jones.

"That does not sound right to me. There are two main groups who suffered in the WW2 Holocaust, one was the Jewish people and two - the Romani Gypsies," he added. A High Court judge found Pickles' policy of calling in Traveller planning applications from independent government planning inspectors and determining them himself to be discriminatory. Even though the policy was found to be discriminatory, Pickles still failed to provide justice to the Gypsy families discriminated against and ordered his government department to not reverse any of his decisions. Less than ten months later Pickles was appointed by the government as the Special Envoy for Post-Holocaust Issues.

The exact number of Romani victims are unclear, but estimates range from between ¼ and 1 million murdered by the Nazi's and their allies during the Second World War. Mike Doherty/TT News 16th April 2018. www.travellerstimes.org.uk.

I recommend the following articles about Eric Pickles in the hope that we all take the responsibility to educate ourselves about such people who hold positions of power over all our lives regardless of our ethnicity, colour, or creed. I dream of a day where the 'collective blame' of the innocent is replaced by holding all wrong and evil doers accountable by their own actions regardless of their position of power, wealth, or social class.

THE MYSTERY IN BEING A GYPSY

The following article, is about Eric Pickles, who had asked the Grenfell inquiry:

"Not to waste his time." The Grenfell Tower firer, which happened in June 2017, had shocked, and devastated the nation. Men, women, and children tragically lost their lives in the North Kensington, tower block firer in West London. The Metropolitan Police are still awaiting the publication of the full inquiry report before presenting evidence to the Crown Prosecution Services to consider if charges will be brought for crimes including corporate manslaughter, gross negligence manslaughter, fraud and health and safety offences. The article can be read online: Eric Pickles asks Grenfell inquiry not to waste his time but gets death toll wrong. The Guardian, 7th April 2022, by Hibaq Farah.

This next article recommendation, again about Eric Pickles antics, is in relation to child sexual abuse, involving teenagers at the Kendall House Home in Gravesend who reported being restrained and experimented on, with huge doses of tranquilizers and other drugs, while living in the care home from the 1970s and 1980s. Some of the teens, who went on to have children, had babies with a range of birth defects. The article can be read online: Sexual abuse survivor who was told to 'adjust her medication' wants Eric Pickles to resign. Guardian-Series, 18th February 2017, Anna Slater (www.guardian-series.co.uk).

Pickles was first elected to Parliament in 1992 and he retired as MP for Brentwood and Ongar at the 2017 general election. He was previously Secretary of State for Communities and Local Government. He was made Life Peer in 2018, and I find this most shocking of all. A Life Peer: is an honour given to individuals under the Life Peerages Act 1958 and entitles holders (in this case Eric Pickles) to sit in the House of Lords under the style and dignity of Baron.

Are people like Pickles in their place of power and authority with the title of Baron because they are compassionate, kind, caring, honest and adequate? Much more importantly, can such people be trusted, after being judged by their 'own' actions?

The way the media condition and dictate to the populous what to think, believe and feel has been nothing less than criminal at times. Weekly, and sometimes daily, there are news reports with the heading: 'Illegal Traveller Incursions' in both the national and local newspapers, containing quotes made by MP's that read, "Travellers blighting the area." The media and members of parliament stand in such a powerful position. Deliberate words like 'incursion' and 'invade' set the bar for their susceptible readers and followers to really believe they are being attacked, by an enemy. After all, 'incursion' by its very definition is a word that evokes fear.

Incursion: an invasion or attack, especially a sudden or brief one: "incursions into enemy territory."

"The media's the most powerful entity on earth. They have the power to make the innocent guilty and to make the guilty innocent, and that's power. Because they control the minds of the masses," Malcolm X.

I agree with the above quote about the media. In my view, media reports are so much more about appeasing their funders and pushing their agenda, usually with a one-sided narrative, than it is about reporting the facts.

As my Granny Dinkey would say, "He who pays the piper calls the tune!"

How many of us are truly interested in those who wield the real power over us all? How many times have we ourselves been guilty of hating or disliking a person solely due to their ethnicity, creed, or colour? And how many of us like, worship or idolise, those who are not worthy of respect simply because they are famous, have a title or in positions of power?

The following article, once again published by Travellers' Times is self-explanatory. I see just one downfall with the reports published in the Travellers' Times, and that's because it's like preaching to the already converted. Mainstream

THE MYSTERY IN BEING A GYPSY

media have the real power; to praise or condemn, to spread love or hate, fear or hope.

The Sun newspaper has apologised to the Romany Gypsy Guild and has disabled all comment threads under Traveller-related articles after complaints about a comment with detailed instructions about 'how to burn out a Gypsy' was posted on a comment thread on the popular tabloid's website. Genty Lee, the founder of the Romany Gypsy Guild, was already in touch with editors at The Sun about racist and illegal comments on their comment thread, when another comment was posted on The Sun website giving detailed instructions on how to murder Gypsies by burning out their caravans.

The commenter explained how burning out caravans was better than shooting Gypsies and also gave tips on how to avoid getting caught. The comment appeared under the article, published on The Sun website on the 9th of October 2018, prompting Gypsy and Travellers to send in complaints. The Sun immediately deleted the comments and disabled the thread so that no further comments could be made. The Sun also apologised to the Romany-Gypsy Guild members.

Genty Lee, (who has been engaging with The Sun for months prior to the incitement to violence comment), told the editors, "This is a wake-up call for The Sun and they should now seriously consider permanently disabling comments when reporting on Travellers." Genty Lee told the Travellers' Times that this was the aim of the Romany-Gypsy Guild to bring about results against racism and that they were also engaging with other newspapers.

From evidence seen by the Travellers' Times, Genty and the Guild have been talking to The Sun in a series of email exchanges since the start of August and have been successful in removing other discriminatory ethnic comments and getting comment threads disabled on previous Sun Traveller related articles.

"Now that a few hundred thousand people have been given step by step instructions to take part in the murder of Gypsies we would like to see The Sun take seriously the responsibility of moderating comments. At the Guild our ethos is 'Educate don't hate'- because we can make a change for our children, grandchildren, and the generations yet to come, while helping each other along the way," Genty Lee told the Travellers' Times.

The Travellers' Times understands that the Sun has agreed to disable all comments whilst they discuss a solution with the Romany-Gypsy Guild.

The full comment, posted under the avatar 'Chelsea Headhunter', said: "Once I had a problem with someone, and we torched their car and home. Problem solved and no they did not all die. It's a very effective treatment for business or personal problems. What would stop you from setting these caravans alight? Police cannot possibly prosecute something like this, you can throw a bottle full of petrol or just pour gas beneath the things at 5 am when they are surely asleep. This is the fastest way to help the gypsies realise it's time to move out of town. Fire is silent and impossible to trace. Shooting makes a lot of racket, especially at night. The same police that work hard to get their Burger King break will be completely baffled by who is setting the fires, not that they would care. Pro tip: do not drive your car to caravan park, either take a bike or borrow someone else vehicle plate. And if you put gas in a can, make sure you do it a few weeks earlier out of town so they don't just rewind the CCTV for the past 2 days and catch you. Also, the caravan's fuel tank is at the back of the vehicle, so make sure you have that part drenched."

(Travellers' Times 7th of November 2018. www.travellerstimes. org.uk).

The above article reported on the ongoing battle we had with 'The Sun online news' that I feel, should not have needed to take place. If we swap the word 'Gypsy' and replace it with any other ethnic group, how long would it take to remove racist comments?

I do not believe that the Sun moderators would have needed alerting to remove it, if the same was written about our Holocaust brothers and sisters, (the Jewish people).

THE MYSTERY IN BEING A GYPSY

Many of us have dedicated so much of our spare time challenging the blatant racism that gets overlooked on media platforms, and I will be the first to admit it gets tiresome because it's relentless.

Yet, if we do not take the time to challenge racism and discrimination, what world do we leave behind for our children and the future generations yet to come?

Even though I have never lived nomadically, nor do I have any family members, relatives or friends who are nomadic either, it still bothered me personally to read articles published using the term 'Traveller'.

Because this term has been hijacked becoming the umbrella term used, within Government sectors and the media, and by professionals to box together completely different and separate people groups. Those who are identified as being 'Travellers' or the 'Travelling community' (in the UK) are Romany-Gypsies, Welsh Kale, Scottish and Irish Travellers, economic travellers, lifestyle travellers, including bargees (people who live on a boat), new age travellers and showmen. This has only served to confuse the already ignorant who do not know that Romany-Gypsies are a legitimate ethnic group.

My local Borough Facebook group was full of angry comments from my neighbouring housed residents, after a recent unauthorised encampment. One comment read, "Why do the Gypsies from our local sites, leave such a state behind whilst travelling around, talk about shitting on your own doorstep."

I chose to engage, with the intent to educate. I called upon the Guild members to join the group chat to help correct false beliefs and together we explained that people who live on permanent sites are 'permanent' residents and not nomadic living people and that the Romany-Gypsies, and Gorgers married in, who live on sites don't move off their own plots to travel a mile down the road, pull up on wasteland, to camp at an unauthorised destination. This is such a ludicrous notion, but it is one that so many choose to believe to be true!

When our local neighbours are not able to differentiate between their permanent area residents and people who come into our area because they are travelling through, their accusation which blames 'my ethnic group' is extremely ignorant on their part. Even more so when holding the residents from my site accountable for disrespectful behaviours, such as the litter left behind after the encampment, where the costs for rubbish removal fall to 'All of Us' as council tax paying residents in our Borough.

It seems to be the most ignorant people, who are the most vocal on social media. Many of whom hide behind anonymous posts. They often make attempts to pass themselves off as being 'Gypsy experts' who has the right to genralise and stereotype about my ethnic group. They each have a story to tell about an encounter they had, or about the bad behaviour they witnessed a Traveller commit. With such stories they go on to condemn my ethnic group. Seldom do they realise the facts are there is a 99% chance that the Traveller unauthorised encampment story they tell, is not about the people from my ethnic group, and they could even be people belonging to their own ethnic group from the Gorger nomadic communities.

When considering that the residents from my site were being blamed for leaving rubbish, and these false allegations were permitted to remain on our area community Facebook group, spreading racial hatred which was displayed in the replies, where several times the derogatory racial slurs (pikey and gyppo) appeared, it is a transparent and disgusting form of 'othering'.

Facebook group moderators are seldom any help with removing racial and derogatory slurs and Facebook themselves allow the words 'pikey and gyppo' to be used because when reporting this, Facebook send back a reply saying, "It doesn't breach their community standards!"

Ignorance is no excuse for allowing racial and derogatory slurs to insult all, as a collective, by ethnicity, creed, or colour.

When Romany-Gypsies and Irish Travellers are commonly conflated as being a single cultural group instead of being recognised as two separate ethnicities - education is

THE MYSTERY IN BEING A GYPSY

lacking. When all nomadic people are believed to be from ethnic minority groups, we still have a long way to go to educate. Were any of us taught within the education system a single thing about the 500 years plus documented English and Scottish history of my ethnic community?

To not know that Romany-Gypsies and Irish Travellers have two completely separate ethnic origins, history and language, and to further not understand the differences between any of the other groups, who are also now termed Travellers suggests that this is self-evident we have always been excluded within the education system.

It's quite something when taking into consideration that there is now DNA evidence that is proving we have been here (in England) for closer to a thousand years, (see: A Romani mitochondrial haplotype in England 500 years before their recorded arrival in Brition). How do we still not have any inclusion within the educational curriculum?

Its erroneous when the masses are left to form their views from what the media drip-feeds to them, or from their own personal views based on personal experiences they have had with a nomadic person, or from what is aired on the TV Gypsy 'mock-a-mentries. It's time for full inclusion within our education system.

16

THE P-WORD

It has become a common occurrence for Guild members to respond to social media posts challenging the discriminatory and racist comments. Especially those on the mainstream media Facebook accounts, as well as the police Facebook accounts. Which are frequently littered with bigoted, and discriminatory comments. It amazes me just how many people use the word 'pikey', openly, and freely, without understanding it's an insulting derogatory, 'ethnic' slur that has been used for centuries towards my ethnic group to insult and offend. Don't get me wrong, mainly all who use the P-Word, do so with the intent to insult. However, I came to learn, the vast majority do not understand the P-word is just as offensive 'to us' as the N-Word is when it is used to insult a Black person. Both of our histories are shrouded with similar targeted racial hatred, with persecution that involves centuries of murder and slavery.

The P-Word has been used for centuries and has been used to insult and taunt Romanies since the 16th century, especially whilst Romanies were being detained at the Turnpikes which also served authorities as a Gypsy data collection point. Restrictions such as curfews were placed on Romanies, who were not allowed to enter villages before and after a said given time.

Please, make no mistake when reading this, and leave no room for personally held stereotypes, because this treatment had absolutely nothing to do with anti-social behaviour or littering. As a matter of fact, my Granny's generation (who largely lived nomadically in wagons) were not guilty of leaving behind any rubbish or mess, nor were the generations before them, and this was true of the 'majority'. To live in an environment that is messy, untidy, or unclean is considered a complete 'ladge up' – it's culturally frowned upon. Even the scorched grass patch, as a result of having a fire,

THE MYSTERY IN BEING A GYPSY

which served as their outside cooker, would be replaced with fresh turf before moving on. Least of all would they dare to leave behind, in my Granny's own words, "So much as a matchstick."

In recent times there's been a new connotation added to the P-Word, which is usually used to insult any person who lives in a trailer (caravan), regardless of their ethnicity. The P-Word is also commonly used to insult by reference to a 'pike fish' which is believed to be an unclean fish. When there are group moderators who understand the P-Word is a racial derogatory slur and they remove the comment, the same commentors will then use the 'pie' emoji followed by the 'key' emoji, to say pie-key in cartoon emojis language. So many times, I can encounter people who believe they are clever and creative for using emojis to deliberately insult or to cause offence. It's actually laugh-able that they believe they are being original.

I can honestly say I have never met an English Romanichal who wouldn't be offended by being called the P-Word. It's a generational reminder of the injustice of 'othering'. This othering has continued right through to present times and it was this same 'othering' that saw the Romany people (Sinti/Roma/Gypsies) in WW2 being considered equal to the Jews, as the number one enemy to the 'cult believers in eugenics' - who were assisted by nazis to carry out the murderous rampage to ethnically cleanse both the Gypsies and the Jews who had been selected for genocide.

The SGTCF had paid for the copyright to show the documentary 'A People Uncounted' in a theatre, as we anticipated large numbers. The showing was held on the International Day of Commemoration in memory of the victims of the Holocaust (Holocaust Memorial Day 27th of January). All the SGTCF committee members supported the event, especially Mark Haythorne who'd put a lot of time and energy into sending out the invites. The 'free' invites went to everyone listed in Surrey in 2016, who worked with Romany-Gypsies. Hardly any of them came to watch the documentary. Maybe the Romanies have been the unrecognised victims of the Holocaust for so long, that now maybe - not many cares enough to want to know.

I was seated in the theatre next to Florentina. Even though I'd only met her once previously, (at the SGTCF conference) I had already gained a soft spot for her. This was something I would have never imagined possible, to like a person who works for the police. But Florentina was different from all the other officers I had met, she knew my world, she understood. Florentina is also a Romany-Gypsy.

I was pleased that both Florentina and Chris Raymer could make the showing with their busy workload. I had held no expectation that they would have the capacity to attend. Chris and Florentina had certainly both committed their time to help make a real change in police relations with ethnic minorities. And I must add, Chris has proved himself to be a real descent man.

Florentina had also become a member of The Gypsy Roma Traveller Police Association (GRTPA) which was established in 2014 by Jim Davies and Petr Torak following a successful employment tribunal case for discrimination against Thames Valley Police. The experience of institutionalised racism led to the formation of the GRTPA that challenges negative stereotypes and discrimination against the Gypsy, Roma, and Traveller officers working within the police force.

Duncan Campbell was the Guardian journalist who conducted the interview with Jim Davies, and in 2024 he told me how the interview came about and what he had learned from it. He shared the following: "I heard about Jim and the organisation from my friend, Gill Brown, who convened the All-party Parliamentary Group for Gypsies, Roma, and Travellers. I had not heard of it before, but I was conscious of the discrimination that still existed in very public form. A Hackney pub near where I now live had a 'No Travellers' sign up for many years and in Islington another pub in a very fashionable area used to have a sign saying, 'Travellers by appointment only'. When I rang that pub and said I would like to make an appointment as I had two Gypsy friends coming up from Wales there was an embarrassed silence at the other end followed by a suggestion that I contact their head office. The sign came down the following day.

THE MYSTERY IN BEING A GYPSY

When I met Jim Davies in the Banbury police station canteen where he was then stationed, the organisation was still quite new and had a membership of 105 police staff across 23 of the 43 forces in England and Wales, and in Scotland. The members ranged from a young Romany dog-handler in Kent to an experienced sergeant in Humberside. Jim told me that there was an old Romany saying – 'Gel on pukker nixes' – which meant 'move on and say nothing', and that that worked for many centuries as a survival strategy but was no longer the case.

Jim had joined the police in 1994, having grown up on a caravan site near Banbury in Oxfordshire. He made a decision to join Thames Valley police, after finding himself unfulfilled by work in a bank and in car sales. In those early days he noted that some officers had an attitude problem and terms like 'pikey' or 'gyppo' were used and there was a general perception of them as criminals. He raised the issue with his senior management, and he got the backing of the Police Federation to take the issue to an employment tribunal at which he claimed he had been subject to racial discrimination through the behaviour of fellow officers. A non-financial settlement was reached, which at that time neither side was allowed to discuss in detail.

In the meantime, he sought out other officers from the community. 'You can think you're the only Gypsy police officer,' he told me, but he soon found out he was not. In 2013, a meeting under the auspices of what was then the Association of Chief Police Officers (ACPO) – now the National Police Chiefs' Council (NPCC) – examined the issue. There Jim met Petr Torak, an officer with Cambridgeshire police, who had come to Britain as a teenager with his family as refugees from the Czech Republic at a time in 1999, when Roma there were being attacked by skinheads and far-right groups. As it happens, I had been working for the Guardian at that time and I was sent to Prague to interview those who were having to flee and to interview some of the children as to why they wanted to come to Britain. I remember being told by some of them that they thought England would be a friendly place to live because they knew and liked 'Mr Bean' and they remembered that Princess Diana was very kind!

Torak, who had always wanted to be a police officer, had spoken little English when he arrived but was encouraged by his father to seek a job in the police and joined in 2006. 'My life mission is promoting the police as a career (to the GRT community),' Torak said who was awarded an MBE for his work with the GRT community. It was at this gathering in 2013 that the idea was born to start the association and challenge the stereotypes. The official launch took place in parliament, hosted by the Labour MP Andy Slaughter.

An email was duly sent to all police forces. Many of those who got in touch were reluctant to be identified. Jim Davies likened their situation to that of gay officers twenty years earlier. Since those days, and the formation of gay police organisations, gay police officers have marched in uniform on gay pride marches and reached the rank of chief constable. Jim Davies said that at that time there were two groups who, on the surface, weren't visible. When he had joined, it was still unusual to be openly gay in the police and what they had achieved had given him a lot of heart. He felt that he might see the same sort of change of attitude and hoped that more and more colleagues would feel free to be open about their ethnic backgrounds.

Prejudice was still common, he told me, whether it was being followed round a store by security staff or being barred from a pub. He showed me a photo of a sign at a Worcestershire caravan site that said: 'No loud music, no Travellers, all dogs must be kept on leads.'

'The police service in general and Thames Valley in particular were very supportive of the association,' Jim said. Mark Watson, a former police inspector who liaised between the NPCC and GRTPA, said at the time that the police nationally were also very appreciative of the new association. Watson said that Trevor Phillips, when he was the chair of the Commission for Racial Equality, had said that prejudice against the community was 'the last acceptable form of racism' and, that sadly, that was probably still the case, so he didn't blame people for being reluctant to identify themselves and he wanted to try and change that. For Jim, Torak and a growing number of colleagues the time when

THE MYSTERY IN BEING A GYPSY

they felt they had to "move on and say nothing" had very clearly passed. At that time, the GRTPA website carried testimonials from serving officers recounting their own experiences. Here are two of them, the first from a former decorated soldier.

Testimony one:

"The month I left the military I visited my grandparents who had stopped at a site, taking with me my prized medals along with the union flag I had brought in a charity raffle held for a friend who died in service. Leaving my grandfather's site I was stopped by the police, they searched my car and upon finding the medal asked me:

'Who have you stolen this from?'

My reply, 'Her Majesty', I reflected the attitude of the officers. Needless to say they appeared rather embarrassed when they found my military ID card and compared that to my name engraved on the side of the medal. Ironic as within less than a week I was about to swap that military ID card for a police warrant card. The examples of racism towards Gypsies, Roma and Traveller people during my time in the police have been frequent, offensive and unchallenged, much to my shame. After eight years of silence, I decided to join another constabulary and be proactive in promoting my heritage. I can honestly say that the people who are aware I am a Gypsy have made no derogatory remarks in front of me."

Testimony two:

"Control room calls up, a shoplifting in progress, two female shoplifters, any units free? Silence. Repeat, shoplifting in progress, any units free to deal, shop staff believe they are Travellers. Suddenly, four units are available and all sorts of people offering 'backup' for two unnamed/unconfirmed women!"

After Duncan Campbell had shared the above, I then spoke with Jim Davies, late January of 2024, and he said, "The reason I took the police to tribunal wasn't just because a few people had used the word pikey or gyppo. It was much more than that. It was because I thought there was widespread systemic discrimination against Romany-Gypsies and Travellers within the police at the time and

I thought I'd try to engage with Thames Valley management to try and tackle it, but I didn't get anywhere – so went to tribunal really as a way of trying to get the problem taken seriously."

All, from any ethnicity, creed, colour, sexuality or religion deserve equal opportunities to climb the ladder of success - within their chosen profession. Only those who are 'incapable' of the skills needed, and for that reason alone, should stay on the bottom rung of the ladder.

There are many professionally successful Romany-Gypsies. But I cannot even produce an estimation for a percentage because largely the majority are not confident or brave enough to disclose their ethnic heritage. Even though I have used 'bravery' and 'confidence', this is only partially accurate because it's much more about having the savvey (sense) not to identify, as we know we are treated fairer, and with respect when hiding our ethnicity in the closet.

Keeping our ethnicity hidden, isn't due to a fear of the unknown, it's a proven and well-documented reality as to why there's a real danger of being victims of discrimination and persecution for having racially identified.

This must change but first wider societies attitudes against us all as a collective, under the term 'Travelling community' or 'GRT community' must be eradicated. We must also challenge people who own 'collective dislike', and 'hatred' for an entire ethnicity because of the few undesirables who can be found in the ethnic majority and all ethnic minorities!

Uncle Joe (Joseph Jones) often says, "There has never been a Gypsy problem, it's always been a political one, that has been created to get us all to assimilate, rather than integrate.

17

GYPSY HOLOCAUST

I took my seat in the theatre and listened to the brave Romany survivors, sharing their testimonies in the documentary 'A People Uncounted'. I sat next to Florentina, who was seated next to Chris Raymer. As soon as the documentary began it showed a tower block, Florentina immediately welled up, she told me the tower blocks where Romany-Gypsies live, in her home country of Romania, are like shantytowns. They have limited or no water and electricity. She said, "Some of my own relatives live in similar conditions."

Listening to one of the Romany survivors recounting her past was particularly harrowing. Looking at the lines etched on her face, every one of them outlined her torment. Her pain and anguish were clearly visible behind her brave words. I felt an overwhelming emotion of sadness that made me cry whilst this survivor was speaking about the revulsions of her childhood.

She shared a memory about herself, and the other deliberately orphaned children, who had eaten human flesh to survive. The nazis had come to their village and shot all the adults, leaving the children without the means to fend for themselves. In sheer desperation of starvation, the children had instinctively consumed the human flesh from the murdered adults. She spoke about the children's despair of being left orphans and watching their parents' bodies decaying and being eaten by wild dogs.

I turned to Florentina for a tissue, and she was sobbing. She laid her head on my shoulder, and I held her tight. We were both overwhelmed at the idea of children having had consumed human flesh, possibly people they knew, or maybe even one of their own relatives; instinctively, to survive because they were starving. I'd never heard of the Romanies' despair during the Holocaust. I knew halfway through the documentary that I would go on to find out all I could about the Romany Holocaust of the Sinti and Roma Gypsies.

Florentina and I were emotionally affected throughout the documentary. When she laid her head on my shoulder, she was truly inconsolable. Her heart and soul felt their pain, just for a moment, as did mine. Listening to their testimonies certainly evoked an inner revulsion towards some members of humanity that I had personally never felt before. All sane people would be saddened, shocked, and disturbed hearing these testimonies but I wondered if Florentina and I had felt the pain of the survivors, of those from our ethnic people, just a little bit deeper.

These so-called scientific professionals, and the aristocrats of nobility who pride themselves in being of 'better' racial, social, financial superior stock only proved themselves, to me, that there's nothing superior about them. They were the ones who should have been annihilated and yet I still cannot condone murder.

They should have all suffered life in the harshest prison on earth, but not because of their ethnicity, religion, skin colour, sexuality or political stance; not for the very same reasons that these monsters have, throughout history, chosen to annihilate innocent elderly people, men, women, children, and babies.

No, they needed to be incarcerated on their own merit, as individuals, according to their own actions. They were cold-blooded, calculated killers, who murdered and enjoyed torturing other human beings, based on an ideology that led them to believe that they were superior. All the while they themselves are the lowest of low. I have not yet found a word suitably fitting for such satanic killers. Due to the actions of these professionals in the fields of science, biology, genetics, criminology, medicine, military, police, doctors, nurses, surgeons, and other authoritarians; I no longer wonder why so many Romanies, worldwide, do not have the 'faith' that most other people groups own - to just "trust the professionals and the authoritarian decision makers".

THE MYSTERY IN BEING A GYPSY

I had heard about the murder of the Romanies, from the stories my Granny's generation had talked about when listening to the rumours their parents had heard. Yet, I had never been taught a single thing about the Romany Holocaust in school. The older generations told horrific tales of their Romany relatives overseas (in Europe) being rounded up, hunted, and shot dead in the woods; leaving behind their children traumatised and defenceless without any adults to care for them. Yet, it had never occurred to me what horrors these children would endure to survive without their parents – I had never heard of their suffering before now. Romanies are the 'People Uncounted' who are seldom recognised or included in the taught history of WW2.

My husband's granny, (Granny Daisy) told me of their families suffering during the war. Granny Daisy's mum was expecting a baby and had given birth whilst her husband was fighting in the war against Germany. She shared this story with me many times. It was a loss and pain that the years gone by hadn't manage to heal. I can still see the pain in her beautiful ocean-blue eyes, every time she would speak about her little baby brother Andrew, who her dad never got to meet. Andrew died from pneumonia at around the age of two. Granny-Daisy told me her mum sent her dad a photo of their son with a lock of his hair, and about how all her family hoped her dad would be home soon. Tragically, when baby Andrew died (from a disease that was a common killer in infants then), her father didn't get granted compassionate leave and wasn't able to return to his family to grieve.

Granny-Daisy said, "When the sirens would sound, they'd all rush to the safety of our nearest bunker. My mother would pick up my baby brother's tiny coffin carrying it to the bunker with us. My mother held off baby Andrew's burial because she was hoping and waiting for the return of my dad. She did this right up until it was confirmed my dad's application had been denied."

To know the history of the of the Romanies persecution during WW2, has taken a lot of time searching for it. There may be a small mention of Gypsies here or there within the readily available written history of WW2; but nothing that reflects the reality.

1 8 1

'A People Uncounted' was an honest account to base my research on. I heard first-hand testimonies from Sinti and Roma survivors whose family's faced annihilation during the 'nazi Final Solution'. Gypsies were targeted in the same way that the Jews were, and yet remain a footnote in history. The effort by nazi Germany and its WW2 allies to commit ethnic cleansing and eventually genocide of the Romany people was dangerously close to being successful.

Genocide: The deliberate killing of a large number of people from a particular nation or ethnic group to annihilate, destroy, the deliberate killing with the intent to eradicate them all.

There was a figure that was used for decades till the early 80s of six million Jews and half a million Gypsies murdered. It's a more telling figure to look at the rate of people who survived then we can really see what the effect was.

An estimated 40% survival for the Jews and an estimated 10% survival for the Gypsies.

There's also very little mentioned about the UK Romany (the Romanichal (Needi's) and the Welsh Kale) who have served in both world wars, fighting for the freedoms we have today. There are no celebrations about their expertise with horses which saw many being needed in the Veterinary Corps. Or any recognition for their skills in hunting, being able to weather the elements, and having an accurate shooting aim. Their life skills aided them in being capable snipers and, in enemy territory, they were an asset to their comrades; especially when it came to foraging for food.

The skills of men who were unfit for active service were also used making cargo nets and slings (large catapults). Skilled tinsmiths were employed for soldering containers and storage batteries. Landscapers felled trees for industrial timbers and for use in the cities. Other's became demolition workers clearing up after the bombings. Gypsy women also played their part. Some joined the Women's Auxiliary Army Corps, drove ambulances, became auxiliary nurses, or went to work in munitions factories, and the rest were hard working in harvesting on the farms to help feed the country.

*My Granny-Dinkeys Grandfather Edward Baker,
10th December 1878 – 18th December 1947.*

There were thousands of concentration camps, throughout Europe that imprisoned Gypsies. Where horrific, harrowing, and intolerable experiments went on within these concentration camps. Professionals carried out their orders received from nazi commanders, as they'd been trained and indoctrinated to do - without questions or protest. I can only conclude they must have been spiritually dark evil beings, who partook in torturous killings that served to excite and fulfil their own perverse evil pleasures, under the guise of scientific human experiments; with their attempts to evidence that nature determines behaviour and not nurture. Their aim was to appease the eugenicist's ideology, and it is my view that many experiments were to try to learn how to create eternal life on earth.

Has humanity changed very much from the atrocities committed during the nazis regime? If we were today faced with media propaganda that filled us with fear and pointed out the enemy who are deemed a danger to us all, are we ourselves capable of turning on our fellow human beings?

It is often said that the nazis had a full list of 'English-Gypsies' for internment. If this is true, then it begs a few questions. Where did the nazis obtain such a list of Gypsy data collection, that is said to have listed all English Romany-Gypsy men, women, children, and babies. If such a list were to be evidenced and made public then it begs the question, "Was such a list voluntarily, or under duress, handed over to the nazi?"

If the above is found to be evidenced one day (because there are still documents that haven't been released), the above questions will taunt me to want to know the answers!

Internment: state of being confined as a prisoner, especially for political or military reasons. Internment is the imprisonment of people, commonly in large groups, without charges, presentation of evidence or a trial. The term is especially used for the confinement "of enemy citizens in wartime".

When 'A People Uncounted' finished, I asked Florentina if she had faced discrimination, within the force, because of her ethnicity. Chris Raymer answered, telling me that they are doing everything they can to ensure Romany-Gypsies are able to excel within the force.

I have passionately given my time to help educate teaching staff about the importance of viewing their pupils as individuals without holding low expectations upon children due to their ethnicity. I am very aware that teachers' low expectation is more common than not. However, I had no idea that this 'low expectation' also exists within the police force, even though I know institutionalised racism exists against us across all professional sectors.

Both Chris and Florentina attended our next SGTCF committee meeting where site issues and police relations were discussed. I had once again asked for members of the Guild to share with me their experiences, but this time about the police. It's extremely important to me that when I attend meetings, I don't turn up sharing only about 'my' friends, and family's experiences. The world is far bigger than me and my lot. I know very well that I have no right to speak on behalf of all English Romany-Gypsies just because we have a shared ethnic heritage. No one has the right to speak for all and there should 'never' be a single person as our appointed representative for any reason, and the Gorger, self-proclaimed Gypsy experts must be exposed as frauds!

There are actually people who stand alone, fraudulently representing Romany-Gypsies, Irish Travellers, and Eastern European Roma (living in the UK), under the banner acronym of GRT. These people, some of whom belong to one of the ethnicities being represented, and then there are others who 'claim' the ethnicity, who are standing on the GRT pedestal.

But it's impossible for me, or any other Romany-Gypsy to represent fairly Irish Travellers and Eastern European Roma (who are first- or second-generation British citizens). English Romany-Gypsy history and culture are completely different to Eastern European Roma, and it has been for around 1000 years, we belong to different tribes. Irish Travellers are a totally different and separate ethnic group altogether.

The pedestal standers are knowingly or unknowingly helping to dilute all three separate groups by being the 'single' representative, which helps ensure that the three groups stay trapped inside a single box, wrapped up in shiny paper under the term 'Traveller or GRT community'. This is being sold as a form of unity and 'stronger together' to fight against discrimination. But this needs to be challenged and brought to an end.

*I am passionate about facts and truths being known.
I believe in living harmoniously together as one race,
'The human race'.*

*However, without knowledge of different ethnicities,
cultures, and creeds, we cannot understand each other, and
without understanding there is no acceptance. Without
acceptance there will never be the respect which is needed
for humanity's harmonious co-existence.*

Respecting all walks of life is paramount. I, myself needed to learn
this, to understand that not all police are brutal thugs in uniform.
I was raised fearing the police, not to trust them, and to never call
them for help for no reason. Because regardless of what is going
on - the police have always shown themselves to be our real enemy.
And this is because there is a long history of police brutality
towards my ethnic group. As well as the anti-Gypsy Laws, Acts,
Legislation and Bills that have been approved and passed from as
far back as the 'Egyptian Act in 1530'.

*Question: Who carries out and enforces the orders of law?
Answer: The police!
They 'follow their orders' regardless of whether the
Laws that they enforce are righteous or unethical.*

I wrote the following in the Guild's Facebook group: "I am
attending a meeting where Police Relations will be discussed. I do
not want to attend as a lone voice, if any of you have any experience
with the police, good or bad, that you would like for me to read out
at the meeting to highlight the things that need change and the
things that are being done well, then please share them on this post,
and I will share your voice."

*I was again completely overwhelmed by the response, which
was of no surprise to me, as being 100% negative. I selected
the following to read out at the meeting within the allocated
time I had been given.*

THE MYSTERY IN BEING A GYPSY

Clair Rice reported: We had a meeting with the DI from the Hertfordshire Police. He reflected upon the policy of 'rousing' a policy which tasked the police to rouse residents of Travellers encampments (the Romany-Gypsies living on permanent sites) in the early hours, every Monday morning. The police would be tasked to turn up note number plates and shine bright lights into every caravan there. They were told how this practice terrified the children. I pointed out that those terrified children are now the adults the police are asking to cooperate and trust in them. The police need to work harder to promote community support, they need to work at building a better relationship. They need to build a relationship where the ethnic group sees them as the protectors and not the aggressors.

And just like the children in my Mum's class, who would have formed unjust negative views about my Mum because of the way her teacher treated her, (who stood her outside the class, on her first day at school because of her ethnicity), I know there are adults who have formed their views about Romany-Gypsies being criminals due to such police policies of rousing. After all, it would be seen as wise to keep your distance from people who are commonly being visited by the police. They must be criminals, right? - Wrong! Just like my Mum in school who did nothing wrong to warrant the treatment from her teacher, the Romany-Gypsies living permanently on these sites, did nothing wrong to warrant the police presence or the treatment received by the police. It was nothing more than an ethnically biased police policy.

Racheal shared: The last time the police visited our site they were looking for a person in connection with a crime. I went out and witnessed an officer speaking to my neighbour abruptly. He said, "Unless you lot get word to him, to hand himself in, you are all going to be raided."

When I heard this, as a law-abiding citizen, I decided to tell the officer that, "I am a 58-year-old woman who has never been in trouble with the police in my life." And I asked him, "Why was he threatening residents because of what a person, who doesn't live on our site, has done?"

He repeated the threat and gave a signal for the other officers to leave. Six police cars came onto our site to threaten us to get word to another person, who we personally did not even know, and this was done simply because of our ethnic origin. I want it asked in the police relations meeting, "Is this right? Is this behaviour acceptable or is it a police discrimination practice conducted due to their ethnic bias's they hold?"

The Police Raids that took place on the sites have traumatized the children, startled the adults, and stressed the elderly. It's been a common practice for the police to turn up in the early hours of the morning, to raid sites, up and down the country.

I have personally witnessed a raid. When my own family lived in Gravesend. The armed force invaded with enough officers to be able to bang on all the residents' doors, and enter their properties, at the same time. Most of these officers would not be sympathetic towards sleeping children or the elderly; neither were the barking, ferocious looking police dogs pulling on their leads. All the residents were woken and made to stand outside their homes – with no consideration given to the weather. The reason given for the raid was: "They were looking for an 'unnamed' person in connection with a serious crime and they 'believed' the person of interest was being protected on the site."

Some officers could be reasoned with when residents would explain, they are not known to the police and their children were sleeping. There were officers who knew the home they were about to raid was not necessary because the law-abiding residents were not harboring an 'unknown' criminal. A few officers showed compassion and allowed the parents to enter their children's bedrooms to carry them out whilst they remained asleep.

THE MYSTERY IN BEING A GYPSY

The police had a 'free pass', without a warrant to raid. There were officers who enjoyed their power trip, and some certainly went the extra mile by opening Chests of Drawers and emptying the content on the floor (the person of interest would have needed to be microscopic in size to be hidden in a Drawer!). And the police who would bang on the door, shouting the threat, "Open up or we'll put the door through," looked as though the residents had disappointed them by opening their doors.

Continuation of the police relations testimonies:

Sara shared: My dad remembers the police kicking the cooking pot over, that was boiling outside on the open fire. The hot water went into my grandmother's face and scalded her. Splatters of the boiling water splashed on his sister as well.

Kathy reported: A few years ago, two police officers came onto my land asking for help because they had locked themselves out of their police car. They'd left the keys in the ignition and the car had automatically deadlocked. It was assumed we would know how to break into their car but disappointingly, for them, we didn't have a clue. I will admit I found it funny watching the police car go up onto a low loader to be towed away. What wasn't funny is that the only reason they came on my land was because they assumed Gypsies must have knowledge of how to break into a car. I have often wondered if they would have been happy to 'overlook', the reason why someone would be able to break into a locked car, to get themselves out of trouble for leaving a police car unattended, with the keys in the ignition! The look on their faces when I told him, "Sorry, I am a dinner lady at our local school and breaking into cars isn't part of my skills needed for cooking children's meals, I can't help you." The officers had no reply to give.

Nathalie Bennett shared: When reporting hate crime, it's never taken seriously, the police seem to only recognise hate crimes if you're a more visible ethnic minority. Many areas do not even record Romany-Gypsy hate crime separately, therefore there seems an unwillingness to recognise it. Growing up, my personal view of the police is one of fear and distrust because of their heavy-handed attitude. I have horrifically witnessed people being beaten by the police. There's a long way to go to build good relations. I have never seen any real good practice, unfortunately only negative experiences and prejudice directed at our ethnic group by the police.

Betty shared: In my experience, the police have never been helpful. I found them to be stand-offish. From my own memories as a child, I can recall being petrified and running away when I saw the police. I am 69 now and when I was eight years old, I remember watching an eviction that had been televised on the BBC where an old man had gone under the wheels of a tractor (he had been runover). My dad would often talk about the police, who came out to where they were pulled. There was a policeman who would repeatedly challenge for the best Gypsy fighter to fight him. They would kick over the cooking pot with our food in it and laugh between themselves. That food could feed a family for two days. After challenging and kicking the food over, too many times to put a number on it, my dad's brother stepped out to fight this policeman. My uncle won the fight against him and for a while the police left them alone in peace.

Rose reported: My mother, who is 84 told me when they were pulled on a layby for a labouring woman to give birth (her cousin), the police pulled up and told them they had to move. They pleaded with the police to allow them to stay just until the baby had been delivered safely. An officer hit the horse, who was still strapped in the harness, making it pull the wagon on. Whilst our relative was inside giving birth. My family were told, "You're not wanted here," and made to move on.

Lisa shared: We live on a site in Kent and the police are regularly parked up, outside the site entrance. They pull over every person coming in or going out to check for tax, MOT, and insurance. How many times do the police really need to stop and check the same vehicle?

Betsy reported: When I was roadside in the late 50s, we repeatedly had stones and rocks thrown at our trailers and motors.

THE MYSTERY IN BEING A GYPSY

Our men decided to stay up through the night to watch, in hiding, to see if they could catch the vandals. Only to find out it was the police doing it. I have witnessed police damage property, brutally beating the men, hitting the woman, and roughing up children. I have had my own children, and other children I know, who were so frightened and traumatised by witnessing the police brutality it affected them emotionally and mentally. One child, in fear, wet themselves because of what they had been subjected to. There are obviously some decent police, but I have never met them.

> *Police and the members of public who kicked over the cooking pots, did so as a common practice that happened throughout Europe. These actions were because of a poisonous myth that accused Gypsies of cooking and eating babies.*

My research has certainly taken me down many rabbit holes, that I didn't even know were there. Horrific histories of ritual sacrifice of babies and children are documented throughout and into present times, but it was never the Gypsies who culturally practiced such satanic, vile rituals. It seemed the more I looked, the more I found out the people from the so-called aristocrat class, those belonging to the cults of eugenics, were the ones who lack compassion and a decent moral code of conduct. Many seem to have only two ambitions, 'wealth and control'. They have gone to great lengths to convince the populous that it's the Gypsy people who are to be feared, but the ruling aristocrats, the 'so-called' elites have been guilty of spreading venomous lies, inventing their own twisted ideologies, backed up in the name of moody, pseudoscience, to stand themselves above all others in positions of control, and it has always been helpful for them to publicise societies scapegoats, which directs the populous to keep looking in the wrong direction.

> *When I collected the police relation testimonies, at the time, I received testimony after testimony about police brutality, and discrimination. I wish I'd have saved them all so I could share them now.*

I understand that the police 'follow orders' that are justified by laws, but we all know there have been many Laws, and there are still Laws in place, that can never be justified which begs the question: "When the police are following orders and they 'know' it's wrong, why do they still do it?"

When the ruling aristocrats and the government have targeted Romanichal's with anti-Gypsy Laws in England it was the police who have enforced those anti-laws. Many times, it's been said, "We are just upholding the law". No! The truth is too many police officers carry out orders that afford them their career, pay and pension.

18

ANTI-GYPSYISM

In between working as a Community Development Officer, I divided my spare time to continue attending meetings and making challenges against the racial and derogatory comments on mainstream media and the police Facebook accounts. Because these platforms often allow racist, bigoted people who discriminate and verbally abuse to have a voice.

There has been a rise in online racism, incitement of racial hatred and death threats, which are openly and regularly made towards Romany-Gypsies in more recent years. The commonly held belief that 'unauthorised' encampments were 'illegal' and the fact that the media have repeatedly been guilty of reporting this falsehood, in their headlines, that read, "Illegal traveller incursion," has resulted in the new common racial slur 'pikey do as you likely'. To many people associate my ethnic group with being a nomadic community, has I have explained several times we are a legitimate ethnic group.

It is automatically assumed that unauthorised encampments are set up by Romany-Gypsies. Unfortunately, far too many believe everything they read or see in the news, and the incorrect belief that trespass was a criminal matter has help reinforce the ideology that Gypsies are criminals who are above the law. In fact, trespass has always been a civil matter until recently.

It was the Police, Crime, Sentencing and Courts Act 2022, where trespass has now since become a criminal matter. Yet, it seems the implications of this Act, for us all regardless of ethnicity, creed or colour has certainly been overlooked because of the hatred openly held against Travellers. Many Gorgers are of the understanding that this Act 'will stop' unauthorised encampments. But the reality is this Act is a door opening for a Law to potentially breach human rights. After, numerous defeats on clauses in the House of Lords, this controversial Act finally came into force on the 12th of May 2022.

The House of Lords initially described this Act as, "Draconian and anti-democratic," but after some concessions were secured from the government, the Bill was eventually approved.

The way I see it, after spending the time to read through the Act, there are many impingements on humanities rights. The freedom to travel, the right to protest and free speech are all brought into question.

Kate Goold, who has decades of experience as a criminal solicitor is on record saying, "Many campaigners and concerned citizens want to express their views without risk of arrest, potential imprisonment or draconian conditions which cause such a restriction to a protest that it almost neutralises the impact. The new Act places greater powers on the police on the ground to determine factors such as noise level before allowing the protest to continue. The arbitrary way in which the police appear to have policed the Sarah Everard vigil and BLM protests compared to other protests, not to mention their bizarre approach to Covid-19 breaches in Downing Street, raises concerns that the balance will be struck too far on the side of those impacted by the protest than on those exercising their democratic rights."

It's distressing that in the 21st century this Act has been passed. Its worrisome how this Bill didn't receive the level of opposition needed, to prevent it from being passed. Was this because people in general have gotten too comfortable with relying on the information the TV news, Newspapers, and representatives of our government report? Do they collectively really dictate to us all how think, feel and what to believe? The 'belief' that trespass has always been a criminal matter has certainly helped this Act to face less opposition than it would have received and the hatred towards Travellers certainly helped this Act not to face the opposition it should have received. Without the following promotion of the Act being widely broadcast: People who set up roadside camps may now face time in prison, a £2500 fine or their home being taken from them, "Would this Bill have faced a stronger opposition?"

People who have experienced unauthorised encampments whereby rubbish and anti-social behaviours occurred are rightly fed up. But it isn't just the lack of respect from those who litter, it's also the injustice felt because we are reminded, at every given opportunity by media, local councillors, and by MPs, "It's our tax paying money being spent on the clear-up." How ironic when we are seldom reminded, by the same councillors, MPs or the media, that it is 'our' tax monies, in the billions, government continuously waste. The Dossier of Waste in the Ministry of Defence 2010-2021', is quite a telling read. Another exposing report can be found on the UK Parliament web site: Government has risked & lost unacceptable billions of taxpayers' money in its Covid response – and must account to the generations that will pay for it, (published on the 23rd of February 2022).

The widespread public welcoming of the Police, Crime, Sentencing and Courts Act 2022, which contains draconian measures to criminalise Travellers, in a supposedly civilised country like ours, would ordinarily be hard to believe. But this Bill has been passed. I hope those who have never read this Act will now go on to do so, because this law doesn't simply target Travellers in a draconian way which many 'believe' will bring an end to unauthorised encampments (it will not!), what needs to have a spotlight shined on it is the real danger of threatening our Human Rights as we know them. The only defence we have as British citizens against tyrants in government is the right to protest. This Act has the potential to infringe on our right to protest but this information hasn't been given to us by MP's, the government or been reported on much in the media.

I am sorry to disappoint with facts, but the reality is even with the New Police Powers the police and council must check on the welfare of the people occupying an encampment, before using the eviction powers. Its criminal that such powers even exist when the simple solution is still, and always has been, a single transit site per Borough or an area for negotiated stopping. I have already begun to see comments, in my local area Facebook groups, where residents complained: "The New Police Powers haven't worked when the council still need to apply to the courts for an eviction notice to be served to get rid of the Travellers."

But those of us who read the content regarding the new Police Powers already knew this! Anyone who holds the belief that the Police Powers will stop encampments – you've been fooled! However, it wasn't the Gypsy or the Traveller who fooled you – it was the elected (or 'selected' depending on which you believe) member of parliament, and the newspaper articles you read that fooled you!

"A lie can always shine brighter in the eyes of them who don't know the truth."

I do understand the frustration both ways, because quite frankly nomadic-Travellers have been used as the scapegoat to bring in the Act, and non-Travellers have been woefully fooled into believing the Act will bring an end to unauthorised encampments, whilst naively trusting the Act will not infringe on their own human rights!

The belief that trespasses has always been a criminal matter has helped form the belief that Travellers are above the law and are able to do what they want. The expectation has been long held by Gorger people that the police should just turn up and mass arrest nomadic-Travellers as soon as there's an encampment. But being 'above the law' couldn't be further from the truth for my ethnic group, (who are termed and placed into the category box of the Travelling community), the anti-Gypsy laws one after another that have been passed, in our country, proves we have always been the victims of the law, not the beneficiaries. And just to add, anyone who really believes the police are frighten and don't come onto sites, they believe in fairy tale rumours!

Through ignorance and bias, permanent Romany-Gypsy residents, who have never in their lives been in trouble with the police or lived nomadically are blamed, threatened, hated, and discriminated against for unauthorised encampments that we took no part in setting up.

The following screen shot below was taken from the comment section on a social media platform that had reported on an unauthorised encampment.

The above comments were featured in the Traveller Times 'Lets Stand Together,' 23rd of May 2019. www.travellerstimes.org.uk.

The commentor (Jon Watkins) used the derogatory term "jippo's" blaming my ethnic group for the unauthorised encampment, without knowing if the people were indeed Romany-Gypsies. The probability of those occupying the unauthorised encampment being English Romany-Gypsies is slim to none. Offensively, his remark compares Gypsies to rodents (by using an image of a rat). This is an insult of the highest order. It relates to the insane ideology that helped bring about the persecution, experimentations, and the murders of Gypsies and Jews in the Holocaust. This level of hate displayed in the above comments, calling for the criminal activity of arson to be committed, which could possibly result in murder, is obscene.

On my personal quest for knowledge, whilst trying to find the answer to my Dad's question, (why are Gypsy people commonly hated world-wide), I came to learn about the cult of eugenics, who are largely to blame for our persecution, enslavement and the atrocities that have been committed against my ethnic community, particularly in the lead-up to WW2, their false belief in 'racial hygiene' during the nazi reign served as the catalyst for the 'hate' and the 'othering' of both the Gypsies and Jews. A hatred so venomous, that the targeted genocide attacks on Gypsies and Jews became acceptable and deemed justifiable. This in return paved the way to see a tolerance held towards the nazis execution of millions, which was accepted by the German masses as being the 'solution to the problem'.

Eugenics: seeks to advance the human race through the 'control' of breeding. Creating a superior society. With only those considered as high-class, being seen as fit enough to breed together, and discouraging, preventing and stopping breeding between those deemed to be the lower classes.

I often ponder a thought, questioning: "Are my ethnic group under threat again?" Is the hatred held by the populous now so deep rooted, and because of the media attention given to unauthorised encampments, the litter, and anti-social behaviour, are we once again in danger of being viewed as 'those people' worthy of atrocities being committed against us?

Just as we became the subject of nazi policy deeming us as 'less human', (the human rats/vermin). My rational thought process tells me, "No, ethnic cleansing to attempt genocide would never again take place, after all, we couldn't all be hated and despised for being viewed as guilty of anti-social behaviours and littering, by default of the category boxes 'Traveller' or 'GRT' – could we?"

What I am sure of is we are certainly all boxed into a single group conflated as being anti-social nomads with no fixed abode, regardless of whether we've ever lived nomadically or not.

The research I have done on my own ethic history has only posed more question than answers. Leading me especially desiring

THE MYSTERY IN BEING A GYPSY

to understand why did people became nazis? Why did they uphold such racist policy? Were they conditioned and completely indoctrinated into believing the Gypsies and Jews deserved the murderous policies invented and implemented against them? Which resulted in them being imprisoned in labour and concentration camps, sterilised and murdered in some of the most inhumane ways thinkable. I can rationalise the possibility that maybe some Germans may have personally witnessed a Sinto or Roma (Gypsy) steal. Maybe some Germans encountered a greedy Jewish person. Which may have, in return, helped them to believe that Gypsies were inbred thieves, and Jews were an economic threat due to their inbred greed. But the public in Germany, who did hold such beliefs, their way of thinking was not entirely own! Such beliefs were predominantly an indoctrination of the drip feeding via propaganda platforms!

When forming views, opinions, and judgements about a person's personality traits and expected behaviours, using only the evidence of either the persons: ethnicity, religious belief, sexuality, political beliefs, skin colour or class - this is a belief which is approving of the eugenics ideology. It's the same false, dangerous ideology that saw innocent people, who had committed no crimes, be executed based on their ethnicity, and targeted by their religious and political beliefs, or sexual orientation, during the Holocaust.

The German people were civilised people, but by the 1940s they were carrying out murder on policy-command. If we try to generalise all nazis as evildoers, it just prevents us looking at the reality of how evil prevails, because this was certainly a social development over a long period of time. The broad masses who aided the nazis by acting as the perpetrators, or the on-lookers who allowed these atrocities to happen, had adopted so easily the poisonous beliefs they were presented with, beliefs such as: they were in danger from the Gypsies and Jews because of their racial inferiority and inbred genetics that cause theft and greed.

So, I wonder are the British people, who have largely adopted the belief that their hard-earned money given over in taxes are being wasted, and the reason they need to pay more, even though they can't afford to – is because of rubbish left behind after an unauthorised encampment?

How many people feel as though they are in danger from Travellers? My thought process cannot help questioning because my ethnic group are included under the term 'Travellers/Travelling community' and therefore blamed and seen the same without having behaved anti-socially, without having littered, without being present at an unauthorised encampment.

Romany-Gypsies (Romanichal: English-Romany), have used the term 'Travellers' since the bronze age in England. Yet, the term Traveller now, is representative of many different and separate people and groups. I fear the ignorance of those who do not know or understand a single thing about the different ethnic groups, cultures, and communities who are 'boxed together' and recognised has Travellers' that even if they were to be educated, it would make no difference towards attitudes of 'collective blame and hate'. Being indoctrinated with a mindset that tars all with the one dirty brush is why so many Germans were easily brain-washed to fear those of us who were deemed racially inferior.

Fear is and has always been a weapon used against people to turn on each other!

I researched to understand what exactly 'racial hygiene' proclaimed, after discovering it has been the catalyst of the hatred held towards my ethnic group and I wanted to understand where this idea originated from and more importantly who publicised it, became the authority on how it worked, and financed this ideology to become so successful that it infiltrated universities, societies, laboratories, and established Institutes within the UK as well as other countries in our world.

The racial hygiene principles have been the driving force behind some of the worst atrocities ever known, one being in Germany that made Auschwitz famous. According to the Holocaust Encyclopaedia, nazi Germany and their allies established over 44,000 concentration camps and incarceration sites in Europe. 44,000! But were any of us taught in school about the Romany

THE MYSTERY IN BEING A GYPSY

(Sinti and Roma) men, women, and children in the nazis camps? Because they were to be found in all of them.

I have been buying a remembrance poppy, every year since the age of 15 when I first began to earn my own money. And I have worn it with pride. Wearing a poppy, I believed, showed I was a civil, kind, and compassionate member of humanity. Believing my poppy badge, on display, united me with those who wish never again to allow evil to prevail. The poppy, I thought, is the symbology on show uniting the good people against evil, regardless of ethnicity, creed, or colour. And in honour of our brave fallen. I wore it for those belonging to my own ethnicity, our British Romany-Gypsy soldiers, who fought against evil. I wore it for every person who defended our country, who were killed in battle and for all the victims murdered in the Holocaust camps. But a reality had dawned, whilst researching - first, we must know it all, to be able to understand, before we can keep the promised reminder of 'Lest We Forget'. I knew only the famous parts about the Holocaust, I wasn't taught about my own ethnic people's suffering, misery, torture, or the murderous rampage that took place against them.

I have certainly come to learn, and I understand, true evil arises to power when good people do nothing and what's even sadder is the realisation the good people who did nothing was as a result of being brainwashed by propaganda.

19

PORAJMOS – THE DEVOURING

The nazi takeover, in 1933, had a totalitarian effect on most things including the boxing world. The Jews were immediately banned from the sport and a ban on Gypsies (Sinti and Roma) soon followed. The eugenicists' ideology was adopted by the nazis who couldn't bear the thought of the people they believed and promoted as 'racially inferior' excelling in boxing. The nazis made sure anyone or anything that could challenge the idea of the 'Aryan master race', was eradicated.

I read about a Sinto-Gypsy boxer called Johann Rukeli Trollmann whose family had lived in Germany for centuries, and how they had hidden their ethnicity; always being careful not to speak their Sinte dialect of our Romani language in public.

The mindset of Rukeli's family, who were German Sinti-Gypsies, is the same as my own family, who are English Romanichal-Gypsies, it is a tradition which was formed many generations ago, prior to the time where we saw the rise of the nazis. Our older generations had already learned and understood we get on better and live a more peaceful life, when hiding our ethnic identity in the closet.

During my childhood, before I understood there are people who hate me because of the ethnicity I was born, I was raised on the perception of fairytales, and held faith in the 'happily ever afters'. The more I read about Johann Rukeli Trollmann the more desperate I became to discover his 'happy ever after'.

The racial inferiority belief, which has been commonly held against Gypsies (worldwide), has existed from at least the time of Darwin through to Hitler, and is an ideology that has somewhat survived into present times also. The hate towards Gypsies has been justified by many unfounded accusations and rumours such as: Gypsies are a people and group not to be trusted because they are traitorous, conniving, and prone to petty crime - which the eugenicists

THE MYSTERY IN BEING A GYPSY

are guilty of perpetuating - even going so far as, producing pseudoscience (moody-science), in their attempts to evidence such claims.

As a result, Gypsies have been excluded socially and faced discrimination and prejudice for centuries, way before the atrocities of the Holocaust. Being socially excluded resulted in Gypsies living in poverty without basic facilities and this can sadly still be seen in many countries today. The Romany who lived (and still live) without the basic human rights of water, simply do not have provisions to be able to live hygienically. Such living conditions are largely overlooked and the worldwide, longstanding, derogatory stereotype that perceives Gypsies as a 'dirty racially inferior ethnicity' is still largely believed.

The story of Rukeli had highjacked my attention (distracting me from trying to find the answer to my Dads question). I found out Rukeli was 8 years old when he first started boxing training at his local sports hall (in Germany) and because boxing is also a favoured sport for many English-Gypsies, it fascinated me to be reading about Rukeli's determination to succeed in the sport.

Boxing had been illegal in Germany because the sport was associated with England - Germany's 'enemy' (during WW1), and when the ban on boxing ended in 1919, many amateur clubs began to open. At the club Rukeli went to he was, at first, shunned by the older German boys because of his ethnicity. But he kept going back and eventually he was shown around the gym. When he finally got into the ring, he was put up against a boy who was much bigger, stronger, and older than him. Rukeli believed he did enough to win the fight, but the judges awarded more points to the other boxer. Yet this still did not deter him. Before Rukeli was 9 years old he'd had three fights and got to the South District Championship in the Bantam weight division. He then went onto win the District Title four times.

Rukeli improved his skills and gained confidence with his unique style of being light on his feet, with skills that saw him landing successful punches whilst avoiding his opponents. His style had no name at the time, but it was more like modern-day boxing than the toe-to-toe fighting of exchanging punches, that was common for that era.

Boxing grew in popularity in Germany and the sport took on political worth. One of the two sports that Hitler wrote about in his book 'Mein Kampf' in which Hitler stated,

"Boxing and jujitsu have always appeared more important to me. Give the German nation six million, sporty and impeccable trained bodies, all glowing from fanatical love of fatherland. Trained to the highest fighting spirit and a national state will come from them, the creation of an army."

Rukeli held the district championship, in his weight division, by the age of 18. He then began to receive financial support which gave him more time to train. As he began to earn money his generosity became apparent, he helped his family, and he was especially generous to children.

In the 1928, Olympic Games the selection committee ignored Rukeli because of his ethnicity, in favour of a fighter who Rukeli had already recently beaten. He then moved to Berlin hoping he wouldn't be ignored, and there he turned professional. Winning his first three professional fights. What mattered in the ring was his performance not his skin colour or his ethnicity.

Rukeli's fame quickly grew, and in the early 1930s he had taken on thirteen opponents and won. He became well known for his 'dancing style'. His handsome looks and new fame also helped to attract women to the sport. Rukeli, was a natural born showman, and he'd throw the ladies kisses from the ring.

In 1932 he became the country's most active professional fighter but the nazis had become the largest party in the national legislation and the Sports Editors of newspapers began to promote the idea of a distinct form of 'German boxing' arguing that the sport must be purified of inferior races.

The nazi controlled propaganda machines (press) then targeted Rukeli based on his ethnicity, and he was increasingly criticised by the media, who dubbed him the "gypsy in the ring," (lower case 'g' is commonly used to show a lack of respect or recognition for our legitimate ethnicity).

THE MYSTERY IN BEING A GYPSY

When the nazis took full control of boxing after they came to power in 1933, they declared that Jews could no longer participate in any way. Not as fighters, trainers, cut men or even doctors. The Jewish boxing champion, at that time, (Eric Seelig) received a letter giving him two weeks to leave the country, which was an escape option that several million other Jews weren't privy to. Understandably, Seelig fled leaving the Boxing title open. Then, in June, Rukeli fought for the title in Berlin. His opponent was a German fighter named Adolf Witt. The nazi officials and spectators obviously wanted Adolf Witt to win because they believed this would help them to prove their racial superiority as the 'Aryan Master Race'.

Witt won the first round but after that it was a 'no contest' with Rukeli scoring repeatedly. Witt tried to land punches but up against Rukeli's swift footwork and defensive skills, he couldn't land a punch. This was an unacceptable show up for a Gypsy to beat the 'so-called' superior-bred German in front of the national press and around 1,500 spectators. Rukeli, a Sinto, a German Gypsy - was winning! In the 6th round of the fight a leader of the national nazi Boxing Association, went ringside to speak with the referee as he wanted the fight to be stopped but there were no grounds to do so. Only the boxers themselves could determine who would win, and Rukeli was clearly winning. But after the 12th and final round the referee called, "No decision."

The boxing fans could clearly see through the political injustice which brought about the decision, and they revolted in uproar. The spectators rose from their seats shouting in protest. Rukeli's manager jumped into the ring, grabbed the scorecards, and showed them around which displayed by every count Rukeli had won. Rukeli just stood in the ring and cried, knowing racism and hate had declared the no decision.

Fights began to break out in the stands, and the spectating boxing lovers ferociously protested the result. The promoters, (who were probably trashed to death) then called for order and made a show of re-considering the scorecards. It was then announced that there had been a mistake and that Rukeli had won the fight: becoming the new light heavyweight champion.

But this result put the nazis in an awkward situation. They had proclaimed themselves the strongest, master race, the most superior nation in the world and they had used boxing as the demonstration to prove their superiority. Rukeli was now the nation's new champion and a member of a dark-skinned ethnicity who the government had ruled to be 'unclean' and a 'danger' to Aryan society. They needed to find a solution to the 'Gypsy problem'. Leaders of the boxing association met and then overturned the result. Their announcement read: the result is cancelled in the fight because of the insignificant effort of both fighters is a fight without a decision. They had declared that Rukeli wasn't worthy of the title because he had cried, and they also fined his manager for disputing with the referee.

A month later, Rukeli dropped to a lower weight class to fight for the welterweight title. The fight had been scheduled by ordering Rukeli: "Fight German-style and do not dance like a gypsy."

Rukeli knew this had been ordered to see he would inevitably lose the fight. As the boxers were called to the ring, Rukeli descended the aisle with a new appearance. He had dyed his black hair blonde; it was so light it was nearly white. He was covered from head to toe in white powder impersonating the look associated with the belief in the Aryan master race.

Rukeli did not lose easily, and by the end of the second round his opponent was bleeding badly. In the third, Rukeli backed him into a corner but in the fourth, Rukeli was knocked down twice and in the fifth round, he was knocked down again and counted out. He had clearly demonstrated he owned a true warrior spirit. But Rukeli had to be stopped by any means because he had shown up the Germans by continuing with his boxing career, even after his unjust treatment.

In June 1935, his license to professionally box was revoked, ensuring the end of his boxing career. He was banned from boxing for 'racial' reasons. Rukeli had to go into hiding to avoid the Gypsy concentration death camps. He was sent twice to the Hannover-Ahlen labour camp and in 1938 to avoid deportation to his death he instead agreed to be sterilised under the diagnosis of 'gypsy congenital feeble-mindedness'.

THE MYSTERY IN BEING A GYPSY

After this, he divorced his Gorger wife to protect her and his little daughter Rita by disassociating himself from them and following the outbreak of war in 1939, he was then drafted into the German army. In the same year, Gypsies were declared as belonging to the 'alien' races. This meant Sinti and Roma were not allowed in public settings like theatres, cinemas, or restaurants. They were no longer allowed to use public transport and were being much more openly targeted in Germany. They were forced to wear a black inverted triangle, (in the same way Jews were forced to wear the yellow star). Such actions taken against both the Gypsies and the Jews was accepted by the public as being necessary because they had been target-selected as 'racially inferior'.

Rukeli was dishonourably discharged in 1942, under racial reasons. After, when he was arrested by the Gestapo, they brutally tortured him before transporting him to Neuengamme concentration camp. The camp was a slave labour brick factory and severely overcrowded. By the end of the year the numbers had increased to around five thousand victims being held there. Rukeli had tried to keep a low profile, but the camp commandant was a boxing official before the war and had recognised him. The commandant then ordered him to train the camp's SS in boxing, every night following his gruelling 12-hour day of hard slave labour. Some of the SS men, who Rukeli taught, treated him with a little dignity by giving him some bread which he took back to the camp and shared out to the children. His health deteriorated, and he was becoming weaker. He had also returned to the camp with a black eye and his inner warrior spirit was burning out.

Rukeli was encouraged by others in the camp to keep fighting, because the bread he earned was keeping the children alive. But Rukeli was growing weaker and was severely malnourished yet despite this he kept going. Until he returned to the camp beaten and broken, the other Sinti men could no longer stand to see him take the beatings anymore. So, they helped fake Rukeli's death, by exchanging his clothes with those of a recently deceased man.

The inmates managed to get him transferred to Wittenberge, one of Neuengamme's satellite camps, but the transfer didn't manage to serve as the escape that it was intended to be. Rukeli was put to work doing some of the hardest jobs in the camp. He was again recognised for his past fame in boxing, and as a result he was made to fight Emil Cornelius, a notoriously evil and feared nazi guard. Cornelius demanded Rukeli to fight him and a crowd of guards, Gypsies and Jews gathered to watch. Even though Rukeli was now skinny, weak, and starving to death, he won against the healthy German. After the fight Cornelius was so enraged and shamed that he forced Rukeli to work all day and then attacked him from behind with a shovel beating him to death.

I had never heard of Johann 'Rukeli' Trollmann before my research. I am not a fan of boxing but having many men in my life who are, I certainly know the names of the greatest boxers past and present. Ali is famous and rightly so, a strong role model and icon for young Black lads to look up to helping them to celebrate their own ethnicity. Just like the history of our Black cousins, ours too is one of enslavement, persecution, and hate – for no other reason than the ethnicity we have been born, and the visual difference of skin colour.

Our ethnic group are equally entitled to have Johann 'Rukeli' Trollmann known as one of the greats. He brought a change to the boxing world that deserves recognition, and he deserves to be famously known. I wish to see Rukeli's achievements celebrated and given acknowledgement (worldwide) both for his boxing career and style which pre-dates Ali. Ali is known for his boxing skill, to hit and not be hit, to "float like a butterfly and sting like a bee", and I take nothing away from Ali, who truly is one of the world's greatest in the sport. I simply wish to see Rukeli have the same fame and recognition of which he deserves. Rukeli should be known, to all boxing fans, as one of the world's greatest boxers, and for being a morally righteous, generous, brave man.

Rukeli's style is widely regarded, by those who know about him, as the beginning of modern-day boxing. I can imagine if Johann 'Rukeli' Trollmann was a boxer in our era, he would have his own catchy phrase and the fame and respect he deserved. He didn't have that fairy tale ending I had hoped for. There is no way I couldn't include his story, after learning about him and I wanted to turn around what was thought to be an insult, made by the nazi press:

"*Rukeli - Danced like a Gypsy King brought class inside the boxing ring*".

Some of the vilest and most evil experiments were executed on the children in the Auschwitz-Birkenau, which was also known as the 'Gypsy family camp'. These experiments were performed on children without anaesthetic. It is soul-destroying to think about their suffering, their pain, and torment before the relief of death came. What type of human in the name of science, medicine, biology, pharmaceuticals, and eugenics could do such things?

These were people, who because of the profession they worked in, they were automatically viewed as having morals, compassion, and humanity's best interest at heart. Therefore, they were held in (undeserving) trust among the populous. They were some of the most excellently educated individuals in the world, within their profession, yet they performed Frankenstein type experiments that involved the mutilation of children who suffered excruciatingly. Even the children's screams, their pain, crying, and suffering were unable to deter Josef Mengele, and the many other physicians from completing their science experiments (or satanic rituals as I see it).

Propaganda and Censorship were crucial tactics used by the nazis for acquiring and maintaining nazi power. The torture, hunting and killing of 'uncountable' Gypsies could not have been carried out without media and university platforms, which the nazi infiltrated with their propaganda. The nazis could have never pulled off such atrocities on the grand scale that they were able to, without the power platform of the media (radios). Indeed, it is true media can be used as an extremely powerful weapon.

"All propaganda has to be popular and has to accommodate itself to comprehension of the least intelligent of those whom it seeks to reach" - Adolf Hitler.

We, the human race, should never allow freedom of speech, freedom of movement or freedom to protest to be restricted in anyway. We each have the right to agree or disagree, we have the rights to hear both sides of the narrative so we ourselves can review all information and in return be 'free' to draw to our own conclusions.

When the Nuremberg trials against the nazi war criminals was held during 1945-1946, no Gypsies were invited to testify.

20

DE-MYSTIFY

In the first week of February 2022, the comedian Jimmy Carr hit all the mainstream media headlines with what's known as 'dark humour'. Carr's show called, 'His Dark Material' was broadcast on Christmas Day 2021.

There were 364 other days in the year on which this could have been released. Yet, on the day that Jesus' birth is celebrated, this was the day Carr's 'dark material' was chosen to be aired. I'm not into any type of 'darkness' but it seemed even more distasteful due to the broadcasting date. The teachings of Jesus are, in my view, a good standard of morals regardless of our religious or faith beliefs. The world would indeed be a better place if we practiced being merciful, loving our neighbour, being peace makers, feeding the hungry, clothing the poor and taking care of the vulnerable.

When Carr's 'dark material' received widespread attention early in February, after a clip about Gypsies in the Holocaust had been shared on social media, I decided to find out what this 'dark humour' was. Carr said, "When people talk about the Holocaust, they talk about the tragedy and horror of 6 million Jewish lives being lost to the nazi war machine. But they never mention the thousands of Gypsies that were killed by the nazis. No one ever wants to talk about that, because no one ever wants to talk about the positives."

There was an immediate back lash. Carr found himself headline news. The Guardian ran with the headline: Jimmy Carr condemned for 'abhorrent' Holocaust joke about Romany people.

Whilst the Holocaust Memorial Day Trust Chief Executive, Olivia Marks-Woldman said, "We are absolutely appalled at Jimmy Carr's comment about the persecution suffered by Roma and Sinti people under nazi oppression and horrified that gales of laughter followed his remarks."

Even Boris Johnson made it publicly known that Carr's dark humour wasn't funny and that it was offensive. It was reported, by several of the mainstream media platforms, that Boris condemned Carr's Holocaust joke about the Gypsies. The Prime Minister's spokesperson said, "The comedian's comments, made during a Netflix stand-up special, were 'deeply' disturbing."

Call me cynical but this comment from Boris Johnson was a red flag for me personally, I just cannot trust that any member of government, or anyone who wields the power, generally cares about a single person from my ethnicity, past or present!

Some people were public in calling for Carr's Netflix show to be cancelled, others called for him to publicly apologise, and many were shocked and offended by this 'dark humour'.

I have never been a fan of Carr so didn't know much about his stand-up comedy or what's written in his books, or the TV shows he has been on either. I searched online for Carr's comedy sketches to understand what exactly this type of 'dark' humour entails. It was a disturbing experience to say the least. Carr's continuous insults, his offensive language (without showing the ability to draw a line), revealed his dark humour was, by design and is 'all' about the shock factor to get people to laugh. Using matters that would ordinarily, for any sane person, never be laughed at, because such matters are disturbing and not funny in the least. Yet, I discovered there are people who can laugh at the vilest jokes made about the worst criminal acts committed, who pay to be shocked into laughing – this is sad to me.

Many of my family members and friends felt that Carr would have never made such a joke about another ethnic group. Whilst I know prejudice and discrimination towards us is still openly accepted, I wasn't sure this was the case when it came to Carr. After learning that Carr really does racially insult all, it seems for Carr if the pounds keep rolling in, that's all that matters; he certainly seems

THE MYSTERY IN BEING A GYPSY

to lack a conscience that would bother most of us if we managed to cause offence or insulted another person or community.

But Carr has built a career from intentionally and deliberately being offensive. His fans have aided him to become one wealthy individual, but I hope his wealth never amounts to be enough for him to have any type of real power. I may well have personally been offended about Carr's Gypsy Holocaust joke, believing his offensive dark humour is only because my ethnic community are easy pickings, if I hadn't learnt that Carr has previously used the Holocaust to joke about the murders of the Jewish people when he said, "They say there's safety in numbers but tell that to six million Jews."

He has also said, "The positive should be taken from Hitler's experiments because he got an awful lot of research done without hurting any animals."

Are his previous 'said jokes' about the Holocaust any less offensive than the one he said about Gypsies? Not at all! Carr himself proclaimed, "It's difficult to say what is offensive because offence is taken, not given."

Yet after making his remark about the Holocaust experiments, he went onto say, "I put it to you if you're not even a little offended, then you didn't really understand that."

Indeed, its true by Carr's own admission that his insults, in the name of having a laugh, are supposed to be offensive. Personally, I find him joking about matters that have devastated people lives, such as the attacks on the Twin Towers in New York, quite frankly, to be sickening. Making jokes about children who have disabilities, I find repugnant, for example, when he said, "People say dolphins are intelligent but that's up against the retarded children we got them swimming with."

Is it any less offensive when he has made jokes about children who have been abused, or suffering with cancer, or the elderly suffering with Alzheimer's?

He has literally made insulting jokes about everything and anyone. Another two examples of his 'dark' humour is when he said, "The average person laughs ten times a day; unless you work in a hospice or with learning disabled adults it could be ten times that." Or when he said, "They say that laugher is the best therapy, so maybe if we keep laughing at people in wheelchairs maybe, just maybe.... well, I'm a dreamer - what can I say?"

I have learned all that I need to know about Carr's 'darkness' his ruthlessness to make jokes about the suffering of others, especially children, is too vulgar for me. People who need to spend their hard-earned money to laugh at such vulgarities, that's their choosing. I do not share their humour, and it's probable I would also not choose to share their company either.

We are all different as individuals, and I truly believe so as long as another's humour, religion, hobbies and behaviours doesn't physically maim, hurt or kill anyone else; this is the attitude needed to maintain living in a free country. This is the reason I wouldn't personally call for Carr's ban or censorship of any kind. I fear in doing so we would be on a slippery slope, going back into a time in history that I wish to be no part of, where people who wield the power will control the populous through censorship.

When Boris Johnson's spokesperson condemned Carr's darkness in joking about the Gypsy victims of the Holocaust, and yet previous jokes about the Jewish victims of the Holocaust have not received such attention, I must question, why?

I have no trust that the government or the media's outcry was because they care that such dark humour is offensive towards Gypsies.

Carr's darkness to joke about atrocities, disabilities, horrific crimes against humanity and debilitating or terminal disease reflects his own level of compassion and his own moral compass. What I wouldn't like to see come out of this though is our freedom of speech to be compromised in any way. I hope my ethnic group will not revolt against such vile, vulgar, and tasteless 'said jokes' by changing our own mind sets becoming in favour of censorship laws. Discrimination and racism are our plight to rebel against, and not just for our own ethnicity, but for all targeted and repressed people worldwide.

Do we really want to live in a world of cancel culture and censorship? Age limits and warning for such 'dark materials'

THE MYSTERY IN BEING A GYPSY

indeed should be put in place but ultimately, we are each our own keepers and responsible for our own lives. I see no good coming from 'big tec companies' and/or from having 'government enforced' censorship.

There's many a true word said in a joke. After discovering how they created these systems of control that allows 'the one percent' to control the masses, I now truly understand the joke of the comedian George Carlin when he told us all, "It's A Big Club and You Ain't In It".

Throughout all my research, I still managed to find nothing evident beyond rumour, suspicion and lies regarding any atrocities committed by Romanies. I found not a single piece of documented history, that told of any evildoings that the Romanies have conducted to deserve the hatred we experience. My Dad, and my own life experiences gave me the passion and desire to discover why we were considered such a threat to the aristocrats and the ruling nobility, who then went on to indoctrinate the masses with their lies that, "We were a threat to the rest of humanity".

This adventure taken back in history has been both emotionally taxing and exhausting at times; but learning my ethnic group have been a peaceful people and have not committed atrocities, leaves me richer for having discovered it all.

When my Romany ancestors first entered England, they were known, identified, documented, and referenced as Egyptians, here in England. The word Gypsy has been used for my ethnic group since as far back has the origins of the word. I would like to highlight that in the England 'Gypsy' isn't a derogatory racial slur.

It is certainly viewed as much in other parts of Europe, but the first English word used to describe Romanies was 'Egyptians'. Our Romany ancestors introduced themselves as having come from 'Little Egypt'. The word 'Egyptian' became 'Gipcyan' which then became 'Gypsy'. There are many English-Romanichal (Romany-Gypsy) who believe we did indeed originate from 'Little Egypt' which was the name of a place in Peloponnese peninsula (what is now Greece), but linguistics and selected DNA results seem to have closed the door on the research of our true origin. I hope it doesn't stay closed for too long!

But even within the UK, English Romany-Gypsies, and Welsh Kale can have different views regarding the word Gypsy. There are those who 'claim' the word and others who never have. But the double barrel 'Romany-Gypsy' is the legally recognised term for us as a legitimate ethnic group. Our historical documentation, spanning over five hundred years of our English history, has been written using Egyptain/Gipcyan/Gypsy.

The word Gypsy has indeed been used, by the insulter, as a derogatory slur and considering how many Laws, Acts and Policies that have been passed against the Romanies which has resulted in murder, branding, enslavement, being experimented on, tortured, and gassed; it is completely understandable why so many Romany worldwide find the term Gypsy offensive.

For me personally, even though I was raised knowing I am an English-Romany, I have no issues ethnically identifying as a 'Romany-Gypsy'. Actually, I love the word Gypsy it sounds so beautiful to me.

There is no denying our ethnic history is one of survival against the odds, one of a great nation who are scattered around the entire world. A people throughout our travels who learned how to survive by their wits. There certainly isn't enough documented about how the Romanies learned and adopted skills and knowledge from the indigenous people from lands they travelled through. Nor is there much written about the knowledge and skills my ethnic group shared on from land to land.

We are a nation who left their homeland, for reasons that can only be assumed, who have supported ourselves using many trade skills, from tin too gold smithing, herbal healing, experts in the arts of entertainment, agricultural skills, horse, and other livestock breeding and training, among many other valuable professions and trade skills, and within the last couple of generations how Romany-Gypsies have successfully become professionals, in all professional sectors, (albeit, largely, by keeping our ethnicity hidden in the closet!).

THE MYSTERY IN BEING A GYPSY

A people who has never invaded, attacked, or attempted to conquer or steal any other indigenous people's land, that's us! That's my people! There is no history of my ethnic community being a political, religious or a military threat to any other race, religion, or country. We have been classified as the unwanted strangers by every country we have been born in; yet the reality is we are rich beyond measure to have every land in the world as our homelands.

Every human being has the right to live life without being victims of hate and discrimination. We must be able to live our lives without fearing exposure of our ethnic origin, without the need to hide our ethnicity in the closet. All people need to be viewed on their individual virtues or lack thereof but 'never' to be judged by the eugenicist's ideology, biased negative stereotypes, or by collective blame. Never should any ethnic group be judged, hated, or blamed for the wrong doings of another person by default of ethnicity.

If only society, in general, would learn to live by two valuable and righteous morals of which I was raised to know:

1. *Treat others as you yourself wish to be treated.*
2. *When judging, do so on an individual's own merit, actions, and heart.*

My book has been written in the loving memory of my Dad Perrin Buckley who inspired me to research. A kind, caring, generous, and righteous man, known to many as 'The Gentleman'. In trying to find the answer to my Dads question, I decided to share some of our ethnic histories that I have learned during my research. And in the hope to make a brighter future against hatred and discrimination this book came together.

This sharing of some of my own ethnic community's persecuted history, that's spanned centuries, alongside my family stories; from my great-grandparent's generation through to my own childhood and adult life, having faced many types of discrimination and hatred that we have endured from all sections of wider society - I hope will go some way to highlight what must change.

That change is to stand against all forms of persecution, apartheid, discrimination, hatred, oppression, segregation, and othering. Which is still a common, and an openly accepted practice, in the 21st Century, against my ethnic group.

We must stand against the perpetrators and for those of us who have been subjected to such wrongs, because we have been born and bred into a world where common views of us is that we are the lowest class of humans - we must recognise that we have been conditioned - through our experiences - to 'shrug off' the hatred, and we have excepted this as 'our normal' because it is all we have ever known.

But this must change and be viewed and challenged for what it is: Racism.

My Dad, Perrin Buckley, a true noble gentleman, in the only character judgment that should ever be counted; the nobility of an individual owning fine personal qualities and high moral principles of kindness, understanding and generosity.